An Introduction to the Study of Christian Missions

by

HAROLD R. COOK

MOODY PRESS

CHICAGO

Printed in the United States of America

2835

To My Wife,
faithful missionary helpmate,
whose love for Christ
and the missionary cause
has never flagged.

PREFACE

THERE ARE MANY BOOKS about missions. Some are the popular kind, such as tales of missionary adventure and the lives of famous missionaries. Others are more scholarly, like missionary histories, surveys, and the studies of missionary principles. But there are not many that give a simple introduction to the whole subject of missions.

I was made keenly aware of this several years ago in helping plan a revised course of studies at Moody Bible Institute. In the subject of missions we wanted an introductory course that would be useful to missionary candidates, and yet would be of practical value to Christian workers at home. This second group especially concerned us. So many Christian workers in the homeland seemed to have so little understanding of missions. A number of our own graduates had told us of their need for such instruction.

Our own experience showed us some things that ought to go into the course. The suggestions of others added even more. I experimented with individual lectures on some of the subjects, with good results. But before the regular classes began, in the fall of 1951, we found that we would have to do without a textbook. None had been written. None, at least, that covered more than a small part of what we had in mind.

Out of that need, and out of three years' teaching the subject to more than a thousand students, has come this book.

Some of the material I have used in other missionary classes. Some sections have also appeared in slightly different form in *Moody Monthly*. But a large part is new.

While the book can be used as a text, I have wanted it to be more than a textbook. I have hoped that it would be useful to a large number of pastors and Christian workers, as well as to missionary-minded Christians in other walks of life. So I have deliberately tried to make it simple and readable. It is an introduction, not a profound study. I have also tried to make it practical by giving specific suggestions for action.

The book makes no pretensions to fine literary style. It is the book of a teacher and a missionary. It aims above all to give instruction. If it shall please our Lord and Saviour to use it in some measure to instruct His Church in its missionary task, its purpose will be fulfilled.

Moody Bible Institute   Harold R. Cook
May, 1954

CONTENTS

7

CHAPTER I

THREE BASIC QUESTIONS

WHAT PICTURE comes into your mind when people talk about missions? Is it a vision of a man in shorts and sun helmet talking to a bunch of naked savages? That's what it is to many people. And we can't blame them. What if it isn't a true picture of most missionary work? After all, it is hard to put missions into a picture. And maybe that picture can serve as well as any other to tell the story of Christian missions.

What story does the picture tell you? You know, we often say that "a picture is worth a thousand words," and "good pictures tell the story." But really a picture tells a different story to everyone who looks at it. It depends on our background and experience. The picture of a mountain lake attracts the artist for its beauty. The fisherman sees it, and right away he wonders how the fishing would be there. But there may be a parent who shudders when he sees it. He remembers a son who was drowned trying to swim in the frigid waters of such a lake. The story is in the viewer as much as in the picture.

What story, then, does your vision of the missionary tell you? Why is he there? What is he talking about? Would you like to be in his shoes? Or do you think the whole thing is rather silly and presumptuous? Does the strangeness of the scene attract you? the romance? Or are you looking below the surface? What is your idea of missions?

Now let me give you mine. No, I ought rather to say, let me

give you the view of the man in the picture, the missionary. What does he think about it? What does missions mean to him? And to that basic question let's add a couple of others that need to be answered. What is the difference between "home" missions and "foreign" missions? And why do some people oppose missions?

What Does Missions Mean?

To the Christian missionary and those who send him out, *missions is the Christian church trying to win others to the Christian faith, especially through a group of selected workers called missionaries.* This is the definition; now let's look at it in detail.

First, we have said that missions is a job of *the Christian church.* We're not talking here about denominations or local churches. We're talking about the great body of believers in Christ who make up His Church. Missions can never be just a private affair. It always involves the church. That's true even of those that we call "independent missionaries." They may be independent of any mission society on the field, but they almost always are sent out by one or more groups of Christians in the homeland. Besides, they always think of themselves as carrying out a task that was given to the whole Church.

Second, we have said that missions is the Christian Church *trying* to win others. In other words, missions calls for deliberate effort. Some people do come into the Christian faith without any person's trying to win them. But they are not often counted as the fruit of missions. In this missions is like selling. You are not a salesman when you simply hand over an item the customer asks for and take his money. You are just a clerk. In the same way, missions is not simply making the Christian gospel available. It's not just saying, "Here it is; you can have it if you want it." It means a job of selling, getting people to want it enough to pay the price to get it.

Third, in missions the Church is trying *to win others to the*

Christian faith. Here's where we'll find some who disagree with our definition. For this means first of all evangelism. But evangelism to the Christian is proselytism to the anti-Christian. He looks at it as a sort of "sheep-stealing."

For example, there are non-Christian countries today, such as India, who would like to have many of the social services of Christian missions like doctors and hospitals. But they object to evangelism. They don't want the people to be converted to the Christian faith. And this is quite understandable. What is harder to understand is those Christians who try to separate the two things. They seem like those who try to help a famished people by giving them food, but neglect to give them seed. The food will help for the present moment, but that's all. Or can it be that they don't see the close connection between the Hindu religion and the pitiful condition of so many of the people?

But we don't need to take time to discuss these objections. Without a doubt, Christian missions in the minds of most people means an attempt to spread the Christian faith. It is the only view supported by the Christian Scriptures.

Fourth, the work of missions is normally carried on *through a group of selected workers called missionaries.* True, there is a vast amount of missionary work carried on voluntarily by members of the Christian church. But they don't often think of themselves as missionaries. They are just personal witnesses to the transforming power of the Gospel of Christ. The work of missions could hardly be carried on without the aid of these voluntary workers. Yet when we speak of missions we almost always think in terms of full-time missionaries.

Notice the word *selected.* For the purpose of our definition the method of selection is not important. The fact is. Even those who argue against the careful choosing of missionaries by a mission board do set up their own standards of selection. Maybe they will simply insist that the missionary be sure that God is calling him to the work. But added to that he will have to be able to persuade a number of Christians to provide his support. The important thing is that in one way or another missionaries are selected workers, selected for the job of missions. And to a large extent the success of missions depends on the wisdom with which they are chosen.

"Home" and "Foreign" Missions

Perhaps you noticed in our definition that we didn't make any distinction between "home missions" and "foreign missions." There is a good reason for it. We don't find any such distinction in the Scriptures. Really they are just two different phases of the same task. The different denominations don't even agree on where home missions ends and foreign missions begins. At least two or three of them carry on their missionary work in Mexico and Central America under a home missions board. Others look at it as a part of foreign missions.

But we're not ready to give up the distinction altogether. Maybe it isn't basic, and we can't find a clear pattern for it in the Scriptures; but it's not contrary to Scripture, and it is practical. It has its real values. Business houses take notice of those values when they have many customers abroad. They usually set up a separate "export division" to take care of the foreign trade. Why? Simply because it brings up a lot of problems that are not found in the home market.

In the same way foreign missions faces many problems not met at home. Let's define home missions simply as *missions carried on within the national boundaries*. Then we can see how it is so. For instance, at home we don't often have the problem of a different language. Nearly everybody speaks English. There are some differences in the manner of living of the people, but it is remarkable how much similarity you will find all the way from California to New York. So we don't have much problem of adjustment there. We don't have the problems with the government that missionaries face in other lands. We know how to live in this climate, and almost everywhere we have access to good doctors and dentists. We can even use older people as missionaries. It doesn't cost so much to put them on the field at home, so if their term of service is short it doesn't mean such a big loss as it would abroad. And finally, we don't have such serious problems of starting a church and helping people to find their place in it.

So the distinction between home and foreign missions is a practical one. Foreign missions calls for missionaries with different qualifications from those at home. They will have to use different methods of work. The range of their activities will often be much broader. Their spirit and their message will be the same, but to be effective they will have to learn and follow different rules of practice.

This is why in these lessons we are going to deal chiefly with foreign missions. To try to deal with both at the same time would in many cases lead to confusion. Some of the principles will apply equally well to both home and foreign missions, as you will readily see. But from this point on, when we speak of missions we are thinking of missions overseas.

WHY PEOPLE OPPOSE MISSIONS

Of course you can expect people who are not Christians to oppose missions. It would be strange if they approved. After all, we don't believe in propagating what we think is not true. We may not mention our disbelief when we are arguing against missions, but it can't help being the main factor. So we're not going to bother with this kind of opposition.

What does concern us more is the opposition from those who claim to be Christians. These are people who say they believe the Christian message, yet they oppose trying to win other people to the same faith. Why?

When we try to find the reasons, we run into some arguments that are really excuses instead of reasons. We could call them "camouflage reasons," because they only serve to hide the real reasons. You will usually hear them expressed with catch-words or phrases picked up from somebody else and glibly repeated. "Charity begins at home" is probably the most common. (As if that meant that charity ought never to leave home!) "Officious meddling" is another term we hear, and sometimes "useless extravagance." It's seldom worth while to refute such objections. They are not the real reasons. But there are at least four basic reasons why many people oppose missions, and we ought to give them some attention.

The first, and perhaps the chief reason, is one that you might have a hard time getting the objector to admit. It is the lack of a personal and vital experience of Christ. It's safe to say that most of the members of our churches in the homeland have never had a deep religious experience. Their parents were members of the church, and at the proper age they too joined. There was no deep conviction about it; it was just the thing to do. Many hardly ever attend church services, but they still count themselves Christians. Others are very faithful to the church, very active in all its affairs, just as they would be in a club.

Now such people find it hard to understand missions. Christianity is good, they will admit. It is even better than other religions. But why try to force our religion on other people? It is rather silly to get so wrought up about religion. Who knows but what their religion is really better for them than ours?

Naturally the one who looks at the church as he would at a club will not be deeply concerned about spreading its ministry to the ends of the earth. Oh, he may be proud of it and speak of it every now and then to friends and acquaintances. Maybe you can even persuade him to give a little help in a membership campaign. But that would be just for the local chapter. After all, membership in the club is nice, but it isn't a life-and-death affair.

How can such people comprehend those young men and women who are ready to bury themselves in out-of-the-way places and give their very lives to win others to Christ? They think it absurd. But the measure of Christ's importance to us is the extent to which we will go to make Him known to others. So we can say that many are not interested in missions because their own faith doesn't mean much to them, and of course it wouldn't be worth much to others.

A second reason for opposing missions is a preoccupation with self. Bluntly put, it is selfishness. It is not the grasping sort of selfishness that tries to seize all the best for one's self. It is a more passive type that we might call self-centeredness. It is the kind that becomes so absorbed in its own affairs that it is blind to the needs of others.

Some of those who oppose missions are more than nominal Christians. They have had a deep religious experience. They are seriously concerned about spiritual needs that affect them personally or touch the local church to which they belong. But when it comes to missions, they say they "just can't see it."

Such a statement is more accurate than they realize. Indeed they "can't see it." The difficulty is the lack of vision in themselves. They see well at short range only. The needs of people beyond their range of sight do not concern them. Nor can they understand why others should feel concerned.

A third reason is ignorance of actual conditions in mission lands. It's strange that we are always objecting that foreigners get a false picture of life in our land from the movies they see. These movies were made right here in this country and by our own countrymen. Yet at the same time we are quite willing to take our ideas of life in other lands from the movies. But they are movies made by our people, and as often as not they are shot right here at home. Some of them are about as far removed from real life in those lands as they can be.

Some of course don't get their ideas from pictures but from books. Then it depends on the book. If the book is fiction the setting may be just as fictional, just as artificial as the plot. If it is a travel book, it still may be fiction. Some travelers are excellent storytellers. Their books are absorbing reading—

but not always true. They write to entertain. They are often able to fill two or three hundred pages with the hastily plucked fruits of a two- or three-weeks' excursion. They don't know the language, so of course they don't know the people. But they can give you their impressions, and they can tell a lot of tales they have picked up here and there—tales that are full of color, even though the colors are false.

The usual author will do one of two things when he writes about natives of other lands. He may picture them as good-natured, contented, childlike people on whom the American traveler looks with condescension. His servants and helpers he calls his "boys." Or he may picture them as altogether vicious, unprincipled rogues, who need to be treated like the villains they are.

With the first picture the author succeeds in giving the impression that missions are actually harmful. The native leads a carefree, happy-go-lucky life until the missionary comes to change his way of living and spoil his Garden of Eden. A young journalist in the South Pacific had such an idea. He saw some young Papuans with black bands around their sleeves and at once condemned the missionaries for teaching the natives "our rotten idea of wearing crape." What he didn't know was that their former practice had been to lop off a joint of a finger whenever a relative died. This was one of the "charming native customs" which the missionaries had changed.

The second picture makes the natives out as hopeless and missionaries as useless. The converts are only clever rascals who impose on the missionary's gullibility. A well-known traveler in Korea was particularly vicious in his written attack on American missionaries there, some years ago. He blamed the missionaries for the disturbances which had taken place in the Orient and urged the government to restrict what he called the "violence" of the missionary enterprise.

In the same book he says of the Korean, "He has neither initiative nor the capacity for work, while he combines in-

temperance, immorality, and laziness in varying degrees."
Then he goes on, "There is, however, an antidote for this state
of things. If sufficient point be put into the argument, and the
demonstration be further enforced by an occasional kick, as
circumstances may require, it is possible to convert a first-class,
sun-loving wastrel into a willing, if unintelligent, servant.
Under any conditions, his dishonesty will be incorrigible."

Would you be surprised to learn that this traveler nearly
lost his life at the hands of the Koreans? His harsh tactics
stirred up a riot among his servants. Before it was over he was
seriously wounded and barely escaped with his life. Yet his
book is still widely read.

During World War II, many Christian soldiers were sent to
mission lands and saw missions in operation. The days of war
may not have been the best time to see what they were doing,
but the men were amazed at the real accomplishments they
saw. They had not expected to see such things. A firsthand
view corrected many of the false ideas they had before. A large
number of them became enthusiastic in their support of missions, and many are themselves serving as foreign missionaries
today.

A final reason for opposing missions is one that, in its older
form, no longer bears much weight. I suppose it is because
people are no longer much interested in questions of theology.
For the reason is theological.

There are two types of theology which are not friendly to
missions. The older one is a type we sometimes call hyper-
Calvinism. In its extreme form it emphasizes the sovereignty
of God to such an extent that man seems to be nothing more
than a puppet. Its classical expression of opposition to missions is in a statement that an elderly minister is said to have
made to William Carey, back in the eighteenth century:
"When God wants to convert the heathen, He'll do it without
your help or mine!"

But there is also a modern type of theology that opposes missions, at least in the sense of our definition. It is a theology that calls itself "liberal" but is so liberal that it can hardly be called Christian. In its view Christianity is not unique. It is not *the* true religion, it is only one of many. And religion is only man's attempt to find God. Other religions are just other roads to the same end. So missionary work is wrong. The religion of other peoples might not suit us, but it fits them. Why unsettle them by trying to get them to worship our way?

We can only remark that if this be called Christianity, it is certainly not the Christianity of the New Testament. Neither is it the Christianity of the historic Church. It is simply Satan's original lie in a new garb.

CHAPTER II

THE NEW TESTAMENT AND MISSIONS

How DID foreign missions get started? Was it a part of Christianity at the beginning? Or did it come later? Did Christ himself have anything to say about it? Is it a necessary part of the faith?

The only way we can answer these questions is to turn to the New Testament itself. In its pages the Christian finds his rule of faith and practice. It is God's final revelation through our Lord and Saviour Jesus Christ. And in it we find the earliest records of Christian missionary work. So we must see what the New Testament has to say.

But in looking at the New Testament there is one error we want to avoid. We don't want to choose just a few scattered texts to prove our point. This "proof text" method has its values. But it is also open to serious objections. It is all too easy to take a text out of its setting and make it teach something it was never meant to teach.

So we are going to consider the broad sweep of New Testament teaching. And when we refer to one passage or another, it will be simply to illustrate the general truth we present. In most cases you won't need the proof of chapter and verse. Instead you will find that a clear view of New Testament Christianity itself will give you the answers you want. You will see that missions doesn't really need justifying. It is taken for granted. In the New Testament missions is the normal expression of vital Christianity.

Of course we don't expect to cover all that the New Testament teaches about missions. The field is too broad. For our purpose it will be enough to show the place of missions in New Testament Christianity.

CHRISTIANITY IS BY NATURE MISSIONARY

The New Testament pictures for us a faith which is by its very nature missionary. In other words Christianity to be Christianity has to be missionary. It is strange that so many fail to see this. That is, it is strange until we realize that many people's ideas of Christianity have only a remote connection with the New Testament.

Many have a false idea about all religion. They think that religion is a purely private concern. It is something like a taste in literature. Some people like serious books, some prefer novels, while others prefer mystery stories and the daily paper. Each one is free to read what he wants, but not to tell others what to read. It is a purely personal matter.

But the truth is that religion can seldom be a purely personal matter, and Christianity even less than most other religions. We grant that faith in Christ has to be personal. It is true, too, that some religious exercises, such as prayer and Bible reading, can be carried on privately. But these are not the whole of religion nor of the Christian faith.

Some countries, such as Spain, have pretended to believe that they are. They have professed to grant religious liberty to minority groups like the Protestants. They have said that everyone is free to believe as he chooses and, in the privacy of his own home, to worship as he pleases. But he may not make any public or even semipublic show of his faith. Neither may he speak of his faith to others. This they call religious freedom. But of course that is only when they are talking of other religions than their own.

Actually there are very few religions that one can profess and practice privately. Such a religion would have to be mostly a matter of ritual, like some lodge ceremonies. It could not change the daily conduct of the worshiper. If it did, it would affect others. Besides, if his religion changed a thief into an honest man, he would have to explain how it happened. Nor could a private religion aim at any changes in society, good or bad. It would have to be a religion content with things as they are. As a religion it would be a sham.

But this is far from true of Christianity. It has a great deal to do with personal conduct. It aims to transform lives. And through changed lives it tries to work changes in society, sometimes revolutionary changes. That is why Christ said that He came "not to send peace but a sword" (Matt. 10:34).

There are many people, too, who have the false notion that religion is a matter of country or race or temperament. The idea is not a new one. The Syrians expressed it in Old Testament times in I Kings 20:23. They said about the Israelites, "Their gods are gods of the hills; therefore they were stronger than we; but let us fight against them in the plain, and surely we shall be stronger than they."

We don't express it quite so crudely today. But we do often say about those in other lands, "Their religion fits them." And some go even farther. Several writers on Latin America in recent years have solemnly affirmed that Protestantism can never take root there because, as they say, it is not congenial to their culture! (Strangely enough, a recent census reveals well over a million Protestants in the one Latin American country of Brazil.)

Now it is perfectly true that some religions by their very nature are limited to one country or people. But this is far from true of all. Buddhism is a small minority movement in India, the land of its origin. Its greatest successes have been in other lands. Mohammedism has fewer followers in Arabia than in lands which Mohammed never saw. It is sometimes called a desert religion; but Indonesia, one of the two largest Mohammedan nations, is as far from desert as it is possible to be.

And when it comes to Christianity, we have a strange phenomenon. It began among the Jews, but most of the Jews have never accepted it. It began in the Orient, but its strongest centers today are in the West. Its Scriptures are very little read in the original languages, but they are read around the world in more than a thousand other tongues.

No, Christianity cannot be simply a matter of private concern. Neither can it be limited to one country, one race, one type of culture. At least not the Christianity of the New Testament.

There are at least two major things that make Christianity missionary by nature: its exclusive claims, and its view of mankind.

First, the exclusive claims of Christianity make it missionary.

The Romans of early centuries and the unbelievers of today both have resented Christianity's claim to be the one true religion. The Romans would have been willing to give it a place among the many religions of the empire. In the same way the unbelievers of today will usually admit that it is, on the whole, a good religion. But they both object to the exclusiveness of the Christian faith. They resent its saying that all other religions are false.

Now there can be no doubt that the New Testament claims exclusiveness for the Christian message. It doesn't picture God as *a* God; He is *the only* God. Paul says, "We know that an idol is nothing in the world, and that there is none other God but one" (I Cor. 8:4). Further, it doesn't present Jesus Christ as *a* savior; He is *the only* Saviour of men. For as Peter said, "There is none other name under heaven given among men, whereby we must be saved" (Acts 4:12). This is the witness of the whole New Testament.

How does this make Christianity missionary? In just this

way. If Christianity is *a* religion and Christ is *a* savior, then my obligation to tell people about Christ and his salvation is relatively small. After all, there are other ways of salvation open to them.

But if Christianity is *the only* true religion; if Christ is *the only* Saviour; if the gospel is *the only* message that can offer men eternal life—then how can I keep quiet? Can I rejoice in my own salvation, knowing that others are dying without that salvation? Must I not feel as Paul did when he wrote to the Romans, "I am a debtor ... to preach the gospel to you" (Rom. 1:14–15)?

Also, Christianity's view of mankind makes it missionary.

When we talk about salvation we mean salvation from sin and from the results of sin. Here is the second reason why Christianity must be missionary. According to the New Testament, mankind is lost, condemned by God because of its sin. "All have sinned" (Rom. 3:23).

Now sin is not a very popular or meaningful word among most people today. To many the New Testament idea of sin is completely foreign. The pagan or the Mohammedan may indeed be familiar with the word, and he may not hesitate to confess that he is a sinner. Because to him, as likely as not, sin is just a matter of ceremonial impurity. He has violated one of the arbitrary rules of his god. So he will have to pay some sort of forfeit to get back into good standing.

But he is likely to view the matter rather lightly. After all, who could possibly keep all the rules of the game without a mistake? Especially when you are not always sure what they are. I am a sinner. So what? Aren't we all?

The idea of sin as moral iniquity, as something that defiles and degrades the soul of the sinner, is not common outside of Christianity. That sin is something that ought not to be, entirely apart from a divine command, is a new idea to most unbelievers. Even where they confess that they are sinners, the sense of "the sinfulness of sin" is lacking.

Our civilized pagans are not much better. They are ac-

quainted with the words "crime," "delinquency," and "error."
But to them "sin" is only a theological term used by old-fash-
ioned preachers and straight-laced killjoys.

Yet unquestionably sin is a major theme of the New Testament—sin and salvation from sin. Sin has alienated the whole
world from God, has corrupted the nature of man, has
brought condemnation and death. No one is free from it; no
one can save himself from it. Only in Christ is there salvation,
a salvation provided by God himself. This is the New Testament message.

If we deny the New Testament view of man and his sin, we
do not need to be missionary. If men, after all, are fundamentally good, though they do make some mistakes; if sin is not
the desperate thing the New Testament makes it out to be; if
its results are not so disastrous; or even if we can plead that
ignorance of the Gospel relieves people from guilt and condemnation; then missions are not imperative.

But no man can fully believe the New Testament picture of
mankind apart from Christ and remain indifferent. If he
really believes it he cannot help feeling constrained to make
the message of salvation known—known to lost men everywhere.

Jesus Christ and Missions

Jesus Christ taught missions. It was not only at the beginning, when He called His first disciples and said, "Follow me,
and I will make you fishers of men" (Matt. 4:19). Nor at the
end of His earthly ministry, when He urged, "Go ye into all
the world and preach the gospel to every creature" (Mark 16:
15). The whole tenor of His life and ministry was missionary.

Look at the purpose of Christ's coming.

Sometimes we hear it said that Paul was "the greatest missionary of all time." Among those who have followed Christ
that is probably true. But greater yet as a missionary was the
Lord Jesus Christ himself.

The New Testament leaves us in no doubt about the missionary purpose of His coming into the world. In fact, this is one thing that makes it different from the birth of any other man. His coming was voluntary, and it had a definite, clear-cut purpose.

The Lord himself told of that purpose when He said, "The Son of man is come to seek and to save that which was lost" (Luke 19:10). Again He said, "I came down from heaven, not to do mine own will, but the will of him that sent me" (John 6:38). And John wrote much later that "God sent his only begotten Son into the world, that we might live through him" (I John 4:9).

Jesus Christ, then, was a missionary, a "sent one." He was sent with a purpose. And that purpose was the same as that of His missionaries today. It was to save those who were lost—those who were "dead in trespasses and sins."

Look, too, at the character of Christ's life.

The character of the life of Christ was missionary in a very real sense. You see, a missionary, like an ambassador, is sent to represent someone else. He has an individuality, but he is expected to suppress it as much as possible. He is not allowed to have a private life. His every act is viewed as the act of the One who sent him. His speeches are not private expressions of opinion but official statements. He is expected to stand in the place of the One who sent him.

Of course missionaries, like ambassadors, forget this once in a while. But Jesus Christ never forgot it. One of the most outstanding characteristics of His life was its utter selflessness. He told His followers that He came "not to be ministered unto but to minister, and to give his life . . ." (Matt. 20:28). And when Paul wanted to back up his exhortation for each believer to "please his neighbor for his good to edification," he reminded them that "Even Christ pleased not himself" (Rom. 15:3).

Even when Christ says, "I am the way, the truth, and the

life," He says it without boasting or egotism. In fact He is exalting the Father, for He adds, "No man cometh unto the Father but by me" (John 14:6). The same is true when He says, "He that hath seen me hath seen the Father" (John 14:9). Actually this last is a clear statement of His missionary character—He stood before them in the place of the Father.

And consider the objective of Christ's ministry.

Some might think that Christ's ministry was anything but missionary. That is, He limited it almost exclusively to those of His own nation, the Jews. On one occasion He told a foreign woman that He was "not sent but unto the lost sheep of the house of Israel" (Matt. 15:24). Yet in answer to her humble faith He granted her request. Also, when He first sent out the Twelve He told them not to go to Gentiles or Samaritans (Matt. 10:5). Yet He Himself ministered to the Samaritans (John 4:5-42).

We need to understand such passages in the light of the whole Gospel. Then we can see how they fit. Without entering into disputed matters of interpretation, we can see two things clearly.

First, Christ dedicated His earthly ministry to His own people, the Jews. On rare occasions He might minister to Samaritans or Gentiles, but these were exceptions.

But, second, even while He was ministering to the Jews He envisioned a world-wide ministry for His Gospel. We see this on numerous occasions, not just at the end of His life.

For instance, in the early part of Matthew (8:5-13), considered to be the most Jewish of the Gospels, we have the story of the Roman centurion's servant. In that case Christ granted the request and praised the faith of the Gentile soldier. Then He added, in a prophetic vein, "Many shall come from the east and west, and shall sit down with Abraham, and Isaac, and Jacob, in the kingdom of heaven." Also toward the end of His life, in the prophecy of Matthew 24 He said, "This gospel of the kingdom shall be preached in all the world for a witness unto all nations" (v. 14).

Whatever the reason, Christ's earthly ministry was to the Jews, but He taught and prepared His disciples for the day when they would take His Gospel to all nations.

And the "great commission" deserves careful attention.

We have purposely waited until now to consider the so-called "great commission." We have done it because so many think of it as the one basis for missions in the New Testament. As a result, if critics cast doubt on its authenticity, the whole foundation for missions seems to be seriously weakened. But we have already seen that missions is a part of the very nature of New Testament Christianity and is taught by Christ himself, even apart from the "great commission."

Christ gave the "great commission" to His followers after His resurrection and before His ascension. It was the one great charge He gave to His Church. There are several accounts of the commission, and it may well be that Christ repeated it more than once. In view of its importance, it would be strange if He didn't. All four Gospels and the Acts give it in one form or another.

The most often quoted of the Gospel accounts are those in Matthew and Mark. Matthew 28:18–20 says,

> And Jesus came and spake unto them, saying, All power is given unto me in heaven and in earth. Go ye therefore, and teach all nations, baptizing them in the name of the Father, and of the Son, and of the Holy Ghost: teaching them to observe all things whatsoever I have commanded you: and, lo, I am with you alway, even unto the end of the world. Amen.

Mark 16:15–16 is shorter and somewhat different:

> And he said unto them, Go ye into all the world, and preach the gospel to every creature. He that believeth and is baptized shall be saved; but he that believeth not shall be damned.

Now recent years have seen a controversy about the final portions of Matthew and Mark. And these are the parts that

contain the account of the "great commission." Critics have
contended that they were not originally a part of those Gospels. It doesn't necessarily mean that they weren't true and
inspired. It is simply argued that they were not a part of those
Gospels as they were first written.

We don't need to go into the discussion here, for we are
not limited to Matthew and Mark. John also has something
to say on the subject. He tells us that when Christ first appeared among His disciples after His resurrection He said,
"As my Father hath sent me, even so send I you" (John 20:21).

Luke also is not silent. He tells us that after His resurrection
Christ joined two disciples as they walked along the way to
Emmaus. They did not recognize Him until He sat down to
eat with them. Then they rushed back to Jerusalem to tell the
others that they had seen the Lord. But in the midst of their
report, Jesus himself appeared and spoke to them. In His talk
He said,

> Thus it is written, and thus it behooved Christ to suffer,
> and to rise from the dead the third day: and that repent-
> ance and remission of sins should be preached in his name
> among all nations, beginning at Jerusalem. And ye are
> witnesses of these things. And, behold, I send the promise
> of my Father upon you: but tarry ye in the city of Jerusa-
> lem, until ye be endued with power from on high (Luke
> 24:46–49).

Again, in the Acts (1:8) we have another often quoted expression of the same "great commission." "But ye shall receive power, after that the Holy Ghost is come upon you: and
ye shall be witnesses unto me both in Jerusalem, and in all
Judea, and in Samaria, and unto the uttermost part of the
earth."

Obviously we cannot deny that Jesus Christ taught missions, that He wanted His followers to be missionary, that He
wanted His Gospel to be preached throughout the world.

CHAPTER III

THE NEW TESTAMENT AND MISSIONS (*Continued*)

THE HOLY SPIRIT AND MISSIONS

IN READING the New Testament we discover that sometimes the disciples did not remember what Jesus had taught them. That was true of His resurrection. Matthew alone tells us of four times when Jesus spoke of His resurrection in advance (16:21; 17:9, 23; 26:32). He also tells us that the Jewish religious leaders were aware of that teaching. When He was crucified, they set a watch to make sure that He stayed in His grave. They didn't want His disciples to steal His body and then claim that He had risen. But they might have spared themselves the trouble. The disciples apparently had forgotten that teaching.

Besides this, they didn't fully understand some of His teachings. They showed it often when He was alive. Sometimes they asked for an explanation, but on at least one occasion they were afraid to ask. And when He died, they clearly didn't understand the meaning of His death. That is, they didn't understand it until after His resurrection. Even then we may question whether they grasped its full significance.

Of course this is what any experienced teacher learns to expect. He knows that those he teaches will not get all that he tries to give them. And of what they do seem to get, they will retain only a part. The inefficiency of the teacher may be partly to blame. But not chiefly. More often the cause is in the pupils. Man's ability to give full attention, to comprehend and then to remember, is quite limited.

From such conditions we would normally expect Christ's teachings to suffer change. No one wrote them down at the time, so it wouldn't be surprising if some were forgotten and others were twisted because of poor understanding or recollection. We would also expect some conflicting testimony about just what Christ did teach.

There are some who, looking at the purely human, say this actually happened. It is the normal thing. So if the New Testament writers agree too closely on any subject, it must be because they depended on the same document or source of information. Such persons emphasize strongly the differences between the Gospel of John and the other three, the "Synoptics." They like to draw contrasts between the theology of Paul and the theology of Peter or James.

This is not the place to go into the arguments they use to support such reasoning. But there is one thing we can say. Without doubt the harmony between the various writings that make up the New Testament is much more remarkable than any supposed discrepancies. That such a varied group of writers, with no official board to check their writings, should present such a unified picture of Christ and His Gospel is astounding. It is this remarkable harmony that calls for explanation much more than any supposed discrepancies.

Of course Christ's disciples had imbibed much from simply being with Him during His ministry. Some might say that they had "caught the spirit of Christ." But as an explanation of the harmony in the New Testament, this falls far short. Those who have "caught the spirit" of a great man don't wait long after his death to differ among themselves. Just look at the followers of any of our modern "great men."

Rather, what the New Testament itself shows to be the controlling factor is a different kind of spirit. It is not an intangible, impersonal influence; it is the Holy Spirit of God. Jesus himself had promised His coming before He died. In fact, Jesus went so far as to say that it was best for Him to leave so that the Holy Spirit could come. He said that He would send Him (John 16:7). He had already told His disciples that part of the task of the Holy Spirit would be to "teach you all things, and bring all things to your remembrance, whatsoever I have said unto you" (John 14:26).

Not only Jesus emphasized the importance of the coming of the Holy Spirit. After He had come, the disciples did the same. The Holy Spirit is so prominent in the Acts that long ago it was said that the book should be called, not "the Acts of the Apostles," but "the Acts of the Holy Spirit." Moreover, in the rest of the New Testament, although He doesn't glorify Himself, the Holy Spirit does take the leading part in directing and controlling the growth of the Church.

FORESHADOWINGS OF FOREIGN MISSIONS UNDER THE SPIRIT

The New Testament presents the Holy Spirit both as the Initiator and as the one controlling factor in missions. He is prominent even in the foreshadowings of that movement. There were at least two such foreshadowings in the early chapters of the Acts.

The first is in Acts 2, where we have the account of the coming of the Spirit upon the believers after Christ's ascension. It is significant that the Spirit came on the Day of Pentecost. Pentecost was the feast which, perhaps more than others, brought to Jerusalem Jews from "every nation under heaven." It was as if the Spirit wanted to make it clear that the Gospel they began to preach that day should reach all nations.

Again, in the eighth chapter we have a most unusual account. We call it the story of Philip and the Ethiopian eunuch. Philip, one of the first deacons of the church, had preached the Gospel in Samaria with remarkable effect. But now the angel of the Lord told him to leave that work and go down to the desert road that led from Jerusalem to Gaza. Here he saw a chariot to which the Spirit directed him. The man in the chariot was a foreigner, an Ethiopian by birth and residence, but apparently a convert to Judaism. Philip led him to faith in Christ and baptized him.

In both these cases there were foreshadowings of a work to come in other lands and among Gentiles who had never professed the Jewish faith. But they were only foreshadowings. The real work among the Gentiles had not yet begun. But even in the foreshadowings it was the Holy Spirit who directed the work.

Five Spirit-directed Steps

In spite of Christ's teaching, the Church did not at first see clearly that the whole world was to be its field. It had to be led out, step by step, into its world-wide missionary ministry. We can distinguish five such steps. They are represented by five crucial acts in which the Holy Spirit played a leading part. We suggest that you read them for yourself in the Book of the Acts. Before the first step was taken, Christianity was limited to Jews and Jewish converts. After the last step it was obvious that Christianity was for the whole world.

Step one: Peter preaches to Cornelius (Acts 10).

The first time the Gospel was preached to a purely Gentile group was when Peter preached in the home of the Roman centurion, Cornelius. Peter had not wanted to do it. His prejudices as a Jew kept him back. It took three divine acts to convince him that Gentiles also could have a part in the Gospel.

The first act was the heavenly vision the Lord gave him in Joppa. Three times in the vision the Lord told him to kill the animals he saw for food. Three times he refused. To a Jew they were unclean animals. And three times the Lord told him, "What God hath cleansed, that call not thou common."

On the heels of this vision came the men sent by Cornelius.

Cornelius, too, had had a vision in which he was told to send for Peter. Before ever Peter saw the men, the Holy Spirit told him, "Go with them, doubting nothing: for I have sent them." So after some hesitation he went.

But going to Cornelius was one thing, and admitting him to the blessings of the Gospel was still another. Peter's reluctance was still seen in his asking why they had sent for him. When Cornelius told of his experience, Peter was partly persuaded, especially in the light of his own vision. But it took a third divine act to seal the whole thing. As Peter explained the Gospel to the assembled group, the Holy Spirit came on them as he had on the disciples on the Day of Pentecost.

This final act of the Spirit convinced Peter. He baptized those who had believed. Later, when the Jewish believers in Jerusalem called on him to explain, he justified himself on the ground that he had only acknowledged what the Spirit had already done (Acts 11:17).

This case was an exceptional one. We never find it repeated in the New Testament. Some have said that it was Peter's use of the keys to open the door of faith to the Gentiles. It was certainly an important act. Its full significance becomes even more evident later, when Paul and Barnabas were called to account for their ministry to the Gentiles (Acts 15:7–11). It was Peter who first opened the door, but it was others who were to bear the major burden of missions to the Gentiles. Peter became rather "the apostle of the circumcision," with his primary ministry to Jews.

Step two: the church in Gentile Antioch (Acts 11:19–26).

Cornelius lived in Judea. We might call it the home field. But Antioch was far beyond the borders even of the northern region of Galilee. It was a Gentile city of great importance in the eastern Mediterranean.

To Antioch the Gospel was brought by refugees. They were refugees from the persecution that began in Jerusalem when Stephen was killed. Wherever they went they spoke of

Christ, and here in Antioch a flourishing congregation of believers sprang up through their witness. Whether any of the congregation were really Gentiles may be doubted. But Antioch was to become the first major center for spreading the Gospel among the Gentiles.

The church in Antioch began independently of the church in Jerusalem. But before long that church took a definite interest in it. To investigate the situation and to establish the believers in their faith, they sent to Antioch an official representative, Barnabas. Aside from having been born abroad, Barnabas' chief qualification seems to have been that "he was a good man, and *full of the Holy Ghost* and of faith."

Barnabas looked over the situation and rejoiced in the evident working of the Spirit. He decided he would stay and help. But he also thought of another helper who would probably fit in very well. Not too far away, at Tarsus in Asia Minor, lived Saul, the man who later was called Paul. Barnabas had been the one to introduce Saul to the church at Jerusalem. Perhaps at that time Saul had told him how that at his conversion the Lord had let him know that he was to work among the Gentiles (Acts 9:15; 26:17–18). When Saul had left Jerusalem, the Lord had said, "Depart: for I will send thee far hence unto the Gentiles" (Acts 22:21). So Saul would be peculiarly fitted to work in a Gentile city like Antioch, and Barnabas brought him in. It was an important step.

Step three: Barnabas and Saul sent forth (Acts 13).

The third step was clearly dictated by the Holy Spirit. "Separate me Barnabas and Saul for the work whereunto I have called them," He said (v. 2). "So they, being sent forth by the Holy Ghost, departed" (v. 4). The Spirit had called the men before. Now the church at Antioch set them apart for this advance missionary work.

We must not misunderstand the significance of what took place in Antioch. The church there was not a modern missionary church. That is, it did not have a mission board or society; it did not set up standards of acceptance for mission-ary candidates nor plan their training; it did not tell them where to go nor what to do; nor did it promise them financial support on the field. But that certainly does not mean that such things are wrong.

What the church did is this. It demonstrated its real inter-est in missions by heeding the instructions of the Spirit and sending forth two of its church leaders and teachers. It went even farther. It identified itself with them and the work they were to do by a sort of commissioning service, the laying on of hands. These were not two individuals acting on their own responsibility; they were sent forth by the church. And to the church they rendered their report when they returned.

Step four: the Jerusalem council (Acts 15).

This fourth step followed the first missionary journey of Barnabas and Paul. In fact, it was a direct result of that step and the preceding one. There were still many who were not convinced that Gentiles could be Christians—at least not without becoming Jews. The issue came to a head in Antioch. Some who had come down there from Jerusalem were teach-ing that the converts had to become Jews in order to be Chris-tians.

This has been called the first really great crisis in early Christianity. It was a momentous one for Christian missions. To use Christ's own figure of speech, it was a case of "new wine in old bottles." The new wine of the Gospel could not successfully be bottled in the old Judaism.

If the Judaizers had been successful, if the converts had been required to become Jews in order to be Christians, it is conceivable that Christianity might still have been mission-ary. But it would have been unsuccessful. The Gospel of Christ is a potent force. It has in itself the power to revolu-tionize men and societies. But when its messengers are weighted down with all sorts of forms and conditions that they have to propagate along with it, their task becomes almost impossible. These Judaizing Pharisees may well have been honest men and sincerely Christian—yet unenlightened by the Spirit. They did not see then what is so obvious today, that a Christianity of the sort they proposed, so closely attached to the Judaism of that day, could never win the world.

But while we may criticize them in the light of today, we need to look out lest we fall in the same sort of error. For it is all too common in missionary work today to insist that people accept not only the Gospel, but with it all the paraphernalia to be found in our churches at home. We are not Judaizers; but we do tend to become Americanizers.

A church council was called in Jerusalem to consider the problem. And the turning point in its deliberations came when Peter gave his testimony of how the Spirit had worked in the case of Cornelius. Since God had accepted the Gentiles on the basis of simple faith in Christ, why should the church try to lay greater burdens on them? To this word was added the testimony of Barnabas and Paul. They told how the Spirit had worked among the Gentiles on their missionary journey.

Then the council gave its decision. The Judaizers were repudiated. The Gentiles should not be troubled in their new faith. The simple prohibitions that the council laid down were in no way a hindrance to further missionary work. Instead, the way was now clear for a greater expansion.

It is important to note that when the council gave its decision it said, "It seemed good *to the Holy Ghost* and to us" (v. 28).

Step five: to the regions beyond in Europe (Acts 16).

Our fifth and final step was taken at Troas. Paul and his companions on the second missionary journey had gone clear across Asia Minor to the northwest. As they moved forward, the Spirit had hemmed them in on the right hand and on the left until they came down to the sea. To go any farther would mean crossing over into Europe. It would be a big step.

This step, too, was guided by the Holy Spirit. Not only had

he guided the missionaries to Troas. In that city he gave Paul the well-known vision of the man of Macedonia. This determined the missionaries to go on over into Europe.

But what did this step mean? It was not the first time the Gospel was proclaimed in Europe. There were probably believers already in Rome. In fact, Paul was soon to write a letter to them before visiting them.

It may have been an indication that Christianity was to turn westward and northward for its greatest successes—to Europe rather than Asia. But take note that the Asia mentioned in verse 6 is not the continent of Asia. It was a province of Asia Minor named Asia, with Ephesus as its chief city. Paul visited it later on this same journey. Perhaps we may say that this was the first *missionary* entrance of Europe—the first time men went there with the deliberate purpose of spreading the Gospel. Other missionaries would soon be following. And Europe was later to be the major center of Christendom.

But perhaps just as important is the fact that this was *Paul*. Not in vain was he called "the apostle of the Gentiles." Not for naught do modern writers call him "the greatest missionary." His work was dynamic and it took firm root. It is not uncommon today to study his work in order to improve our own. His work was intensive, yet it became much more extensive than that of others. No man has left a greater mark on Christian missions than Paul.

Now Paul's ministry up to this time had been in western Asia—especially in Syria, Palestine and Asia Minor. His original home was in southeastern Asia Minor. There were many Greeks in Asia Minor, but it was still different from Europe. A water barrier separated the two continents, but with it there seems to have been also a barrier in thinking.

At least in Paul's case this seems to have been true. When the Spirit led him to sail across to Macedonia, it appears that in his thinking the last barrier to a world ministry was passed. He didn't stop in Macedonia. On down into Greece he went.

He conceived a great desire to go on to Rome. He wrote of this to the church at Rome and mentioned that he would like them to help him on his way farther west to Spain (Rom. 15: 23–24).

The first step toward a full proclamation of the Gospel among the Gentiles was taken when Peter preached to Cornelius. The last was when Paul went to Macedonia. And all along the way it was the Holy Spirit who was directing the movement.

CHAPTER IV

THE NEW TESTAMENT AND MISSIONS (*Concluded*)

MISSIONARY WORK BY OTHERS THAN PAUL

MOST PEOPLE tend to think of Paul and his companions as the only missionaries in the New Testament. Some have gone so far as to consider Paul the standard, the norm, and to disregard others entirely. This does violence to the truth, regardless of what we may think of the values of Paul's example for us today. Paul may have been the greatest of the early missionaries, but he was far from the only one.

We have an advantage in speaking of the missionary work of Paul. We know more about it. Not only do we have a long section of the Acts devoted to his work, but we also have a collection of his own letters. On the other hand we know comparatively little about the missionary work of the others.

That the twelve apostles were intended to be missionaries, and that most of them did become missionaries, is hardly open to question. Their very title "apostle" is nothing but the Greek form of the word "missionary." They did stay around Jerusalem for a long time, perhaps until the council described in Acts 15. In that chapter "apostles and elders" are mentioned. But by the time of Paul's last visit to Jerusalem, it appears that all the apostles had left the city. Acts 21:18 says only that "all the elders were present." Whether more than one of the apostles may have died by that time we have no way of knowing. Of course James, the brother of John, had long before been executed by Herod (Acts 12:2).

About Peter we do know a little. While Paul calls Peter "the apostle of the circumcision," that did not keep him from being a foreign missionary. Paul himself tells us of Peter's being in Antioch (Gal. 2:11). He was even fellowshiping with the Gentile believers in that foreign city. In fact, Paul says he scolded him for withdrawing from the Gentiles when certain Jews came up from Jerusalem.

We can't be sure whether Peter ever visited Corinth, in Greece. It doesn't seem very likely. Yet he did have an influence there. It was such an influence that, when the church began to split into several factions, one of the parties claimed to be Peter's party (I Cor. 1:12).

Furthermore, Peter's first epistle implies that it was written from the foreign city of Babylon (I Peter 5:13). This is not at all strange. Even though Peter ministered chiefly to Jews, we know that there were many Jews in that eastern region who never returned to Palestine after the captivity.

It is true that Roman Catholic writers claim that by Babylon Peter really meant Rome. This is largely because they want to find in Scripture some proof of their claim that he was the first bishop of Rome, the first Pope. However, in either case he would be a foreign missionary. Also, though the tradition is much disputed, there is a story that he was martyred in Rome.

The Scripture gives us little information about the later ministry of John. It seems clear that he and Peter were both in Jerusalem until the time of the Jerusalem council (Gal. 2:9). But after that we are not sure. The almost universal tradition is that he went to Ephesus, a mission field, where he ended his days. It also says that it was from Ephesus that he was exiled to the island of Patmos, where he received the Revelation.

If we have little information in the New Testament about

the later ministry of Peter and John, we have even less about the rest of the Twelve. The Syrian Christians of South India claim that Thomas went to India and established their church. The claim has enough basis to be given serious consideration by historians. There is also a tradition that Matthew went to Egypt and Ethiopia. And there are other traditions concerning others of the Twelve. Some of the traditions are plausible; others are later inventions and obviously false.

From all the evidence that we have, the most that we can say is that all of the apostles except James appear to have become foreign missionaries.

But besides the Twelve there are also other missionaries mentioned by name in the New Testament.

We have already said something about Barnabas. He occupies a prominent place and appears to have been the actual leader of the first missionary journey with Paul. It is interesting to notice that he is called an apostle in Acts 14:14. He parted company with Paul after an argument about taking Mark along on a second trip. Barnabas may have been influenced by the fact that Mark was a relative, but later results seem to show that his judgment was sound. Paul himself, toward the end of his life, wrote to Timothy, "Take Mark, and bring him with thee: for he is profitable to me for the ministry" (II Tim. 4:11). But of Barnabas' later ministry, all that we know is that he returned to Cyprus.

Silas we know as Paul's second partner on his missionary journeys. Timothy and Titus were younger men whom he associated with himself in his missionary work. The epistles he wrote to them might be called "letters to younger missionaries." They tell us a little about these men, and also something about the missionary principles and methods in which Paul instructed them.

Luke, a physician, accompanied Paul for a time. Just how often or how long, we don't know. But his greatest service was in his writing. He wrote one of the four Gospel accounts. In addition, he became the first missionary historian in writing the Book of the Acts.

Paul and Luke both tell us of others who did missionary work, such as Apollos, Aquila and Priscilla, Demas and Tychicus. But we get only fragmentary glimpses of them. We wish we knew more.

Of this we are sure. The missionaries whose names we know are only a small portion of the great company of missionaries who, in New Testament times, carried the Gospel to a large part of the Roman world and beyond. Who first preached the Gospel in Rome? We don't know. Who established the church in Alexandria, metropolis of Egypt? We have no idea. What were the names of those who began the work in Antioch? They are not given. Yet these were three of the principal cities of the empire.

It is clear that there were many Christians engaged in spreading their faith to other lands. A large part were humble witnesses whom circumstances had taken to those lands. But there was a vitality in their faith that made them proclaim it wherever they went. There were others who, whether on their own initiative or under commission from a church, devoted their lives to this task of missions. And, as in the case of any good work, there were even some false missionaries. Paul found it necessary to warn against them on at least one occasion (II Cor. 11:13.)

Conclusion

In conclusion we may state with certainty that the New Testament is a distinctively missionary book. All the authors of its various parts were missionaries, with the possible exception of James and Jude. In fact, almost without exception the books appear to have been written in a foreign language— Greek. In only one or two cases is it seriously suggested that a book may have been written originally in Aramaic, the language of the Jews of that day. As far as our earliest copies are concerned, they are all in Greek.

The epistles of Paul were all written to missionary churches or to younger missionaries, except the one to Philemon, who was a member of a missionary church. James and Peter both wrote to Jews, but to the Jews abroad. The Revelation was written for the comfort and encouragement of missionary churches. And of course the Acts is primarily a missionary account. Luke's previous book, the Gospel, was written for Theophilus, whose name is Greek, whether he is a real person or only stands for the Greek-speaking believers.

All in all, we cannot escape the conclusion that New Testament Christianity is essentially and intentionally missionary.

CHAPTER V

THE OLD TESTAMENT AND MISSIONS

W HEN A MISSIONARY wants to give the people among whom he is laboring the Word of God in their own tongue, he begins by translating some part of the New Testament. This is perfectly proper, for it is in the New Testament that we have the message of Jesus Christ our Saviour. The culmination of God's revelation to man is Jesus Christ. And these are the books that tell us of Him and of the salvation that He wrought. So then, although they have translated some parts of the Bible into well over a thousand languages, most of these have only the New Testament or a part of it.

Now the missionaries do not mean by this that we should entirely neglect the Old Testament. Doubtless none of them would be willing to say that the Old Testament is any less the Word of God than the New. If it were possible to give the people the whole Bible, they would not withhold any bit of it. This is true even where the reading of the Old Testament might raise some questions difficult to explain.

There are few who would go as far as did Ulfilas, the great pioneer missionary to the Goths in southeastern Europe. You may remember that Ulfilas provided the first translation of the Bible into any Germanic tongue. But he refused to translate the Books of the Kings. His Goths were already too inclined to warlike deeds. He was not going to provide them with any further encouragement or excuse from the Bible if he could help it.

But most missionaries today do not shun to declare to the people "the whole counsel of God" insofar as they are able. Polygamous Africans are even allowed to read the story of polygamy in the Old Testament. Still it is true that missionaries, as well as preachers here in the homeland, cannot avoid dwelling much in the pages of the New Testament, with their rich exposition of the life that is ours in Christ.

Even in choosing a text for a missionary message to the folks at home, a text which often serves only to give a sort of Biblical introduction to our story of life and Christian service in another land, we usually turn to such passages as Acts 1:8 or Romans 10:14 and 15. Only occasionally do we refer to some passage in the Old Testament. Is it that the Old Testament is lacking in missionary character? Not at all. It doesn't indeed have so many brief, to-the-point texts that can readily be used to introduce a missionary talk. But its missionary character is readily apparent to those who become familiar with its message.

Now in studying the missionary character of the Old Testament, there is one thing we want to avoid so far as possible. It is the same as in our study of the New Testament. We don't want to choose certain proof-texts from here and there, pulling them out of their context and arbitrarily putting them together to prove our thesis. We want to seek honestly for the message that the Old Testament itself has to give us.

Three questions stand out for which we want answers. Let me state them briefly to begin with, and then come back to deal with each one in detail. First is the question, "Does the Old Testament have a *missionary message?*" That is, does the message of the Old Testament have prime significance not only for the Jewish people, and not only for the age in which it was written, but also for other peoples and for other ages? Does its message have a vital importance for us today? Does it concern peoples whose culture differs as widely as that of the Russians and the Japanese?

Our second question is this, "Does the Old Testament show a *missionary purpose?*" That is, does it show that it was God's intention to have its message known among other peoples besides the Jews? It is not always easy to show intent. God doesn't always reveal clearly just what His ultimate purpose in any case may be. But we shall see what revelations of His purpose we may be able to find in this regard.

And for the last question we would ask, "Does the Old Testament reveal any *missionary activity?*" That is, was there before the time of Christ any attempt to bring the blessings of the Old Testament revelation to others? We can readily understand that the Jewish nation as a whole might overlook its missionary responsibility. Hasn't the Christian church done the same thing for long periods of its history? In fact, aren't there many Christians today, in spite of the clear injunctions in the New Testament, who say they don't believe in missions? But our question is, "Was there any comprehension of a missionary responsibility among those who had the Old Testament revelation? And was there any attempt to fulfill this responsibility, whether by direct evangelism or in some other way?"

Now let us return to our first question:

DOES THE OLD TESTAMENT HAVE A MISSIONARY MESSAGE?

A missionary message, of course, is *a message that one has and another needs*. It is a message that ought to be propagated, spread abroad.

Just what is the message of the Old Testament? Clearly it is more than just history and law and poetry and prophecy. These are what we might call the "literary values" of the Old Testament. But its greatest value is the message it seeks to give us. The author of the Epistle to the Hebrews is referring to the Old Testament when he says in his opening verse, "God . . . hath . . . spoken." And about what has He spoken?

First of all, He has spoken about Himself, the beginning and the end.

And what is the Old Testament message about God? Here some unbelievers will say that there is more than one. They will object that the God of the prophets is not the same as the God of the law. They try to reconstruct the development of the idea of God in the Old Testament according to their own notions. Jehovah was at first a tribal deity of a wandering group of Bedouins. Then, as the Jewish nation emerged and grew, they needed a broader concept. So their crude, harsh and primitive ideas gave way to the more advanced views of a later day. Of course this is simply the old evolutionary hypothesis carried over from biology to religion.

But we are not going to follow these fanciful reconstructions. Rather we shall see in broad terms what the Book says.

Our first picture of God is that of *the Creator of the universe*. We ourselves are so familiar with this concept that we fail to grasp its significance for others. We think it rather trite.

Now it is true that many heathen do have a more or less vague idea of a creator. But others do not. When Paul preached his famous sermon on Mars Hill in Athens, he saw fit to begin with, "God that made the world and all things therein" (Acts 17:24).

What a message this is to the millions who still fear the spirits of rivers and trees, mountains and lakes, animals, birds and other creatures! "There is an almighty God over all, a God who created all things!" "The heavens declare the glory of God and the firmament showeth his handiwork" (Psalm 19:1). Is not this a missionary message?

Closely allied with this picture of God is that of *His oneness*. God is one. This uniqueness of God is the substratum of the whole Old Testament from the Law through the Prophets.

It is on the basis of this teaching that Mohammedan missionary work has been built and has had its great successes. "There is no god but God!" Man in his rebellion against God has invented a multiplicity of gods. But now he groans to be delivered from these demons of his own creation. What a missionary message, to be able to assure men that they do not need to try to placate a horde of capricious, evil-working spirits! There is one God, one only. It is the one who created all things.

Third, the Old Testament pictures *God as righteous*. Again there are some who think this is trite. "Of course God is righteous," they say; "otherwise He wouldn't be God." But this is only an indication of what effect the Bible has had on their thinking. Even those who profess unbelief are affected by its teachings. For where did they get the idea that God is righteous?

The heathen gods are not righteous. That is, they are not righteous in any moral sense. They can only be considered righteous if we admit that anything a god does is right simply because the god does it. The pagan gods are deceitful, immoral, licentious creatures whose only law is their own caprice.

Many speak of the stern justice of the God of the Old Testament as if it were unattractive and unbecoming. They do not realize how even this would be a great relief to the followers of pagan gods. The pagan gods are like Oriental despots; their very whims are laws, and what is right today may be altogether wrong tomorrow. "How can you know?" their followers ask. "How can you be sure what the god wants?" What a relief to worship a God whose demands are always right and just!

But in the fourth place *God is also merciful and compassionate*. All through the Old Testament His justice is balanced with mercy and compassion. We see it even in close association with His judgment. We see it in the covenant He made with Noah and all mankind right after the flood (Gen.

9:15–17). We see it in the Law, "showing mercy unto thousands" (Exod. 20:6). We see it in the Psalms and in the Prophets (Ps. 119:64; Mic. 7:18). How the world needs this mercy and compassion!

Finally, the Old Testament shows us a *God who is sincerely interested in His creatures, especially in man.* There is nothing farther from the Old Testament view than the picture of a God who created the world, established its laws, "set it going, and then went fishing."

It is not only in such New Testament passages as John 3:16 that we find God's concern expressed for mankind. It is found throughout the Old Testament. Even in the special covenant He made with Abraham (Gen. 12:3; 18:18; 22:18) and repeated later to Jacob (Gen. 28:14) He did not fail to mention the blessing it would bring to all the world.

Second, God has spoken about man.

The Greek philosopher who urged, "Know thyself," expressed a deep truth. We don't know ourselves, but we need to. We need to know our capabilities and our weaknesses. We need to know wherein we are like others and wherein we differ. We need to know what can be expected of man—what forces move him.

The first thing the Old Testament tells us about man is that *he was made in God's image* (Gen. 1:26, 27).

There are some unbelievers who scoff at this. They laughingly say instead that "man made God in his own image." But false as their statement is, it is still not so ridiculous as you might think. For if man had to invent a god he couldn't do better than make him in the image of man. After all, what higher nature has he ever known? With all his weaknesses and his failures, man is still the crown of creation. He is the only creature who has been able to bring much of the rest of creation under some measure of personal control. No wonder the Psalmist wrote, "Ye are gods; and all of you are children of the most High" (Ps. 82:6).

Now it is not easy for us who look on the outward appearance to see God's image in man. Sometimes we find it particularly hard. There are some in whom it seems to be disfigured more than usual. We ourselves fall far short of God's perfection, yet we tend to despise those others who seem to be a little farther away from it than we. We magnify their inferiority to us, forgetting the old adage of "the pot calling the kettle black."

We talk about racial superiority. We used to speak of "the white man's burden." We agree with the Latin American, who looks down on the Indian as an inferior creature and proudly speaks of himself as a *racional,* a "rational being." We even talk sometimes about the uselessness of missionary work among backward peoples. And all because we refuse to believe the truth we find at the beginning of the Old Testament: that man, as man, was made in God's image.

Closely related to this first teaching is the Old Testament doctrine of *the unity of the human race.*

The Old Testament does at times distinguish between families and tribes and nations. But our modern racial discrimination is completely foreign to it. It is true that there are some who try to justify their racial attitudes by an appeal to the Old Testament. There are a few who still call attention to the curse that Noah pronounced against Canaan, the son of Ham (Gen. 9:25). They say that because of that curse all Negroes must forever be servants.

But such teachings don't come from a study of the Old Testament. Instead, they are born of our prejudices. And because we want to believe them, we try to find some basis for them in Holy Writ. In all honesty we ought to call them rationalizations.

What the Old Testament does clearly teach is the unity of the human race. We all have a common ancestor. In him we all were made in God's image. By descent from him we all are brethren. Each has followed his own willful way, and some have prospered more than others, but in nature we are one —one even in our sins.

Men always have resisted this idea of the unity of mankind. Partly it is because of pride, the sort of pride that makes a prosperous man deny his poor relations. But even more it is because it means responsibility. If all mankind is one, then every ruler is responsible to his people, the noble to the commoner, the privileged to the less privileged. They are all of the same stuff. Then, too, those in foreign lands who don't have the blessings that we enjoy in Christ do have a just claim on us. It doesn't matter that their race and culture are different from ours. They are still of the same blood.

But the Old Testament is also a message about *man's sin*.

Like a great mirror, the Old Testament reveals to us our hearts. And what we see is not altogether pleasant. It is not a cause for pride. Even the best of us are guilty. Sin has corrupted all of mankind.

The heathen gods are nearly always arbitrary and capricious. Their commands are seldom based on what is of itself right and good. As a result, sin among the heathen comes to be not much more than ceremonial defilement. It is not impurity of heart but of body; not violation of conscience but of rules.

But in the Old Testament sin is revealed as moral iniquity. Before ever the Law was given, in the days before the flood, "the imagination of the heart of man" was evil, and God condemned him. Sin existed apart from the Law. It was not the Law that made it sinful. The Law merely pointed it out and condemned it.

Now the Law did establish for the Israelites certain forms and ceremonies. But they were never intended to be an end in themselves. Isaiah 1:11–17 shows how useless God held them to be by themselves. "To what purpose is the multitude of your sacrifices unto me? saith the Lord . . . Wash you, make you clean; put away the evil of your doings from before mine eyes; cease to do evil; learn to do well . . ."

Not only among the heathen but in all the world today this message is needed. Even in Roman days it had a great attraction for pagan idolators. The Old Testament told of a standard of righteousness that was unchangeable, a righteousness that was in the very nature of things. So numerous Romans and Greeks became converts to Judaism. They felt the need for such a message.

Besides this, the Old Testament pictures sin as universal among men. No one is free from its contamination. All are sinners and need to be redeemed from sin. How strangely this contrasts to the idea that many hold today—the notion that primitive peoples lead a happy, childlike existence, unaware of sin until the missionary comes. Not only is this far from the Old Testament teaching, it is the most absurd sort of fiction. Only overromantic Americans, ignorant of the realities of heathenism, could imagine such things. For however perverted his ideas of sin, the heathen is always conscious of its presence.

And the Old Testament also reveals sin as that which separates men from God (Ps. 14:2–3). That is the burden of its message: sin separating man from the source of life; God seeking to reconcile man to Himself that he may live again. This indeed is a message that is needed—a missionary message.

But again, the Old Testament message is also a message of salvation and hope. From the entrance of sin, in Genesis 3, to such wonderful prophetic utterances as Isaiah 1:18, this message is repeated in innumerable ways. "Though your sins be as scarlet, they shall be as white as snow."

Who could keep such a message to himself? Who could believe the reality of such a hope and not make it known to others?

We could go on and show other details of the Old Testament message that are missionary. We find, for example, that the Old Testament is concerned with the fundamental problems of all mankind, and not just those of one group. Its appeal is so universal that people everywhere forget that its leading characters were Jewish. They think of them in terms of their own race and nation. This universality of appeal makes it a missionary Book.

Then, too, there is no question about the missionary character of its prophetic message. The prophets often forgot national boundaries as they carried out their ministry. It was too big, too vital to be limited to one people, even the "chosen people."

But we don't believe it is necessary to go farther. The message of the Old Testament clearly has a missionary character.

CHAPTER VI

THE OLD TESTAMENT AND
MISSIONS (*Continued*)

W<small>E HAVE SPENT</small> a great deal of time with the missionary *message* of the Old Testament. If the message is missionary, then it is not necessary for us to get other evidence to prove that the Old Testament also has a missionary *purpose*. Yet we can plainly show that, too, from the words of the Old Testament itself.

Look at the opening chapters of Genesis. Man sinned, and immediately God made known what was to be the channel of His redemption. But as we read the story in chapter 3 we realize that this is not to be the redemption of just a single man or group of men. God's plan embraces the whole of humanity. He purposed to provide a salvation sufficient for all mankind.

Again, in chapter 4 we have the account of the first murder. But with it we have the foundation for that very sense of missionary responsibility that Paul expresses so forcefully in Romans 1:14. God questioned Cain about his brother. Cain burst out rather petulantly, "Am I my brother's keeper?" And many a modern follower of Cain has tried to shrug off responsibility in the same way. But God still thrusts aside that flimsy excuse. He still wants to hear from us the acknowledgment, "I am debtor both to the Jews and to the Barbarians; both to the wise and to the unwise; so as much as in me is, I am ready to preach the gospel"—I am ready to tell everyone the good news of God's redemption.

The first eleven chapters of Genesis have to do with the whole of mankind. It is not until chapter 12 that the scope is more limited. Then we have God choosing one man, Abram, and his descendants to stand in a special relationship to Himself. The Hebrew people are to be the channel of His revelation and of the salvation that He is going to bring to the world.

But even in choosing Abram, and in making a special covenant with him, God didn't lessen His vital interest in all men. Look at the way He states His promise to this man of faith. Every time He repeats it He mentions that He proposes in this way to bring blessing to the whole world. "In thee shall all families of the earth be blessed" (Gen. 12:3); "all nations of the earth shall be blessed in him" (Gen. 18:18); "in thy seed shall all the nations of the earth be blessed" (Gen. 22:18). When He renews the promise to Jacob, He says the same thing, "In thee and in thy seed shall all the families of the earth be blessed" (Gen. 28:14).

In the Book of Exodus we have the beginning of God's special dealings with the Hebrew people, as He tries to make them into a nation to fulfill His purposes. We see Him called "the God of the Hebrews," as if He were a purely national deity. His great final purpose in choosing them is nearly lost to sight. It is subordinated to the immediate program of welding them into a nation and bringing them into possession of the promised land. When He gave the Law to the people at Mount Sinai, the Ten Commandments did begin with a reminder that the God who was speaking was the same one who had created the universe. But the Law itself and the covenant were given to them as a people distinct from the rest of mankind.

Still, even in the Law we don't entirely lose sight of the final world-wide objective. In Numbers 14:21 God says, "As truly as I live, *all the earth* shall be filled with the glory of the Lord."

Again in Deuteronomy 10:14–19 He reminds the Israelites, "Behold, the heaven and the heaven of heavens is the Lord's thy God, the earth also, with all that therein is. Only the Lord had a delight in thy fathers to love them, and he chose their seed after them, even you above all people, as it is this day . . . For the Lord your God is God of gods, and Lord of lords." And lest they should get haughty because of this great privilege He adds, "Love ye therefore the stranger: for ye were strangers in the land of Egypt."

Of course when we come to the prophets the consciousness of God's missionary purpose becomes very strong. Perhaps no one expresses it more beautifully than Isaiah. In chapter 49:6, God speaks to his servant the Messiah, and says, "It is a light thing that thou shouldest be my servant to raise up the tribes of Jacob, and to restore the preserved of Israel: I will also give thee for a light to the Gentiles, that thou mayest be my salvation *unto the end of the earth.*"

And in another Messianic passage, chapter 52:13–15, God says: "Behold, my servant shall deal prudently, he shall be exalted and extolled, and be very high. As many were astonied at thee; his visage was marred more than any man, and his form more than the sons of men: so shall he sprinkle *many nations;* the kings shall shut their mouths at him: for that which had not been told them shall they see; and that which they had not heard shall they consider."

Does the Old Testament show a missionary purpose? Who can doubt it? Even in the choosing of the Hebrew people that missionary purpose stood out. As one writer has put it, "The choice of one race among many was not an antimissionary act on God's part, selecting one and letting others go by; it was rather among the most missionary of His acts, choosing one and filling it with a sense of His will and deep understanding of His nature so that it might teach all mankind that nature and that will. God's elections are always for the channeling

of blessings. The favored group that forgets this will soon lose
the favor."

MISSIONARY ACTIVITY

Our third question is an interesting one, and one that deserves more careful study and attention than we are going to
be able to give it. Does the Old Testament reveal any missionary activity? Was there any attempt to bring the blessings
of the Old Testament revelation to others? Did those who received the revelation comprehend its scope? Did they realize
that it was for all men? Were the descendants of Abram conscious of their God-given task?

It is very evident that a majority of the people didn't have
any such consciousness. In the minds of many doubtless the
idea of the extension of the message was identified with the
idea of the expansion of political Israel. The benefits to be
had through a knowledge of the true God were for those who
became Jews.

This is not a strange idea. In fact it is all too readily understood in the world today. A common accusation against the
missionaries of Christ in many lands is that they are tied up
with their governments. They are held to be spies or advance
agents of American or British imperialism, either politically
or economically.

But if the Old Testament has a clear missionary message
and purpose, there must have been *some* appreciation of the
call to a more unselfish ministry. In some cases we know that
this was true. Whatever other lessons we may get from the
Book of Jonah, for example, we know that it is a definitely
missionary book. The prophet's message was not a pleasant
message. He was a very unwilling, and later a disgruntled missionary. Yet a missionary he was, and that in the distant As-
syrian city of Nineveh.

Still, such examples of missionary activity are comparatively rare in the Old Testament. Such men as Daniel did

make God known in other lands; but little is said about any large-scale attempt to win others to His worship.

In spite of this lack of information about missionary activity in the Old Testament, we know that some was carried on before the time of Christ. Christ himself speaks of the strenuous efforts of the Pharisees "to make one proselyte" (Matt. 23:15). Also there were numerous proselytes, or converts to the Jewish faith, who came to the feasts at Jerusalem, as on the day of Pentecost (Acts 2:10). So there was some recognition of missionary responsibility, even though it was very little in comparison with the later Christian missionary enterprise.

For it is in Christianity that missions reaches its peak.

CHAPTER VII

MOTIVES AND AIMS OF MISSIONS

B EFORE WE TALK about the particular motives and aims
that we ought to have in missions, we need to understand
our terms. We often confuse the two words, motives and aims,
both in our thinking and speaking. We use them to mean just
the same thing.

Now a motive is something that prompts one to act. It is
the force that impels us to do what we do. It may be considered as answering the question *Why*.

An aim is an objective, an end in view. It is what we expect
to accomplish through our action. It may be regarded as answering the question *What* or *To what end*.

What brings the two into such close association that they
are hard to distinguish is this: sometimes the purpose to be
accomplished by our action is so desirable in itself that it
moves us to act. The motive force then is the force of attraction. It is the force of the magnet instead of that of the rocket.
It is the sort of power that a prize has to make men exert themselves more than they ever would through a sense of duty.

In this chapter, however, we are going to try to keep the
two things distinct. To get at the motives we want to ask,
"Why do people want to be foreign missionaries? What reasons impel them to offer their lives for Christian service in
foreign lands?" We are going to keep it on this personal level,
which is basic, rather than talk about the church's motives.

We need to answer these questions. In one way or another every young person who volunteers to serve Christ in the foreign field has met them or is sure to do so. Sometimes those who ask the questions are scoffers—those who have no real comprehension of Christianity and can't be expected to understand its world ministry. But just as often they are professing Christians, some of whom would sincerely like to know. Then sometimes, too, it is the candidate's own heart that wants a clear-cut answer.

If you are thinking of foreign missionary service, you want to evaluate your motives carefully. There is perhaps no other type of work where your motives will have so much to do with your success. Romantic notions, the desire to travel, the "lure of the exotic," the purely emotional response to a stirring missionary message—all these are motives. They may even be strong enough to get some young people out to the field. But their weakness shows up just as soon as the young missionary comes face to face with conditions in an unfavorable, even actively hostile heathen environment. They won't keep you going.

A Chinese writer, now teaching in an American university, has commented on the ineffectiveness of many modern missionaries to China. He says that one of the main reasons is that missionaries today don't have the strong motivation that earlier missionaries had. Maybe some of the early missionaries were not as well educated as they should have been, but they had an overpowering sense of divine mission that overcame all obstacles.

There are some today who with their superior knowledge criticize and even ridicule those early missionaries. They made many mistakes, we are told. They held to a theology that is outmoded. They attacked the pagan faiths indiscriminately, without appreciating the good features to be found in them. They sometimes became dictatorial. And according to modern standards they committed many other errors.

Yet at the same time some of these critics, alarmed at the confusion, uncertainty and lack of real effectiveness today, have urgently called for a re-examination of the basic principles of missions. And of course that involves motivation. But any amount of study is not enough. Study can clarify motives, but it can't generate them. And the missionary, to be effective, must have something fundamental, something deeply compelling to thrust him out—something such as what the apostle Paul experienced when he wrote, "Woe is me if I preach not the gospel!"

In the experience of most successful missionaries there are two motives that seem to stand out as more compelling than any others. First is a keen realization of what we have in Christ. It is the consciousness that in Christ we have what the whole world desperately needs. We have a message and a life so eternally valuable that the whole world ought to have them.

When a man is *sure* that the way of Christ is not only a better way but is the *only* good way; when his experience of Christ has transformed and ennobled his own life; when he faces heathenism frankly, realizing its awfulness, but at the same time realizes that it can be changed by the same Saviour who changed his life; he cannot help feeling the constraint of missions. Such a motive, such an inner constraint, is not only enough to send him to the field; it will also sustain him in the midst of difficulties and discouragement.

There is a second motive, closely related to the first. It is simply the command of Christ. Of course, for one who has never acknowledged the Lordship of Christ His command has no force. Neither does it have much force in the life of one who has never learned to obey. But the one who wholeheartedly has submitted to the authority of Christ, who finds pleasure in seeking to do His will, or even feels strongly the sense of duty to his Lord, finds that this motive is a strong one. It may even be sufficient of itself. No other reason is needed, such a one decides, for the Lord himself has commanded, and it is for His servants to obey.

These two motives have generally proved to be more compelling than any others. But we don't mean that there aren't any others. There are many others. In fact, it is doubtful if any of us can completely analyze his motives in all their complexities.

It is difficult to know just how much of the spirit of adventure enters into the decision of some young people to be missionaries. Others have been led to think that full surrender to the Lord necessarily means foreign missionary service. Sometimes a young man wants to serve the Lord, but he doesn't think he can qualify as a preacher or a teacher. So he thinks he may find in foreign service a place for the abilities that couldn't be used at home.

Where missions send out short-term missionaries for teaching, some may look at it as an opportunity for getting some experience. In the case of missionaries' children, they sometimes simply follow in the footsteps of their parents, doing a work with which they are already somewhat familiar. And we might add that some young people are moved by an appeal to youthful idealism and by an altruistic desire to help humanity. For young people are still idealists.

These and many other motives may or may not play a part in sending a missionary to the field. Even where they do, they do not need to be condemned. What we need to recognize is that they are inferior motives. They don't have the powerful drive or the sustaining force of the two principal motives. At best their place is secondary.

Now it is the motives that determine the aims of foreign missions. The man who is moved only by compassion for human suffering will feel that his ministry is done when he relieves that suffering. His aim is to heal sick bodies, to feed the hungry, to give shelter to the homeless, to stop unjust oppression. But the one who is moved by a sense of obligation to make known the Gospel goes much deeper. It has meant life to him. His aim is to see that Gospel brings the same life to others in other lands.

In greater detail, we may say that the true missionary of Christ has one great aim, in two phases: to witness to Christ in such a way that (1) men will put their faith in Him, and that (2) the Church of Christ will be established and built up. This aim is entirely spiritual, as it should be. Did not Christ say, "Seek ye first the kingdom of God, and his righteousness; and all these things shall be added unto you"? (Matt. 6:33). And the aim includes both evangelism and teaching.

Notice that we do not say that the one aim is "to preach the Gospel." Such a statement is as shallow as it is inaccurate. The missionary cannot "deliver his soul" by delivering the message, regardless of results. He is more than a herald who merely repeats the words he is told to repeat. The missionary is a witness—a witness who is deeply concerned that others shall believe his testimony and render a favorable verdict.

Preaching is important in missionary work. It is a prime way for presenting the message and seeking to persuade men to accept it. But the preaching must be in terms that men can understand; it must be with the sincerity born of experience; it must show a warm interest in those to whom it is directed. And preaching is only one way of witnessing. There are many others.

We have said that the true missionary has one great aim. This does not mean that he may not have many other related aims. It simply means that the others will be subordinated to this one principal aim.

For instance, he will heal the sick and feed the hungry, but not as an end in itself. It will be as an expression of the life of Christ which dwells in him. He will teach the illiterate, that they may come to a better understanding of Christ. He will introduce new ideas, new practices, perhaps in a few cases a new civilization. But it won't be because he thinks these things are in themselves of prime importance. It will be because they are necessary to the full expression of the life of the Saviour. All his purposes will center in the one great purpose, and from it they will all derive their significance.

Perhaps the greatest weakness in Christian missions today comes from a deviation from this one great aim. Our mission schools continue to bear the name of Christian long after they have lost sight of any distinctively Christian objective. Our social services become so involved in the physical and the economic that the spiritual is omitted or given scant attention. We become interested in promoting *our* mission, *our* denomination, *our* movement, and forget the Saviour and *His* Church which *He* bought with *His* own blood. We content ourselves with making modest progress toward some minor objective, not noticing how far short we fall of the main goal. Even when we don't actually turn aside, we tie ourselves up with trivialities.

God grant us a clear vision of our objective!

CHAPTER VIII

WHOSE RESPONSIBILITY?

UPON WHOM does the responsibility for missionary work rest? Up to this point we have not considered such a question. We have not differentiated between the obligation of the individual and the obligation of the Church.

But just who is responsible? Is missions the responsibility only of those individuals who feel a special interest in such a cause? Or should missions be considered the responsibility of the Church as a whole? Sometimes we have acted as if it were the enterprise of just a select few, some of whom have gone as missionaries, while the others volunteered to support them in their work. Is this as it should be?

This individualistic attitude is perhaps more prominent to-day than ever before. You can see it in the large number of independent missionaries who try to start and carry on a work unconnected with any denomination or church group. You can see it in the rapidly growing number of independent missions. They get their support from interested individuals in a large number of churches, but they are not in any way subject to the control of those churches.

You can see it, too, in the attitude of many young people who offer themselves for missionary service. They look on it only as the fulfilling of a personal obligation. They have no thought that they might be called to represent a larger fellowship, the Church. In modern political terminology, they think of themselves as "personal representatives" of Christ rather than "ambassadors" of Christ and His Church. Are they right?

When we look to the New Testament for the answer, we find two answers. Rather, we should say that the Scriptures teach that both the individual and the Church are responsible. And there is no clear marking out of the responsibility of each one. In a way, it is like the responsibility of several men who have signed a note for a mutual friend. When the note is due, if the man can't pay it himself, the creditor can demand payment of all the signers jointly, or of any one of them individually. That is, they may all get together and pay the note, each one giving his share; or any one of them may be made to pay the full amount. Each one who signs the note makes himself responsible for it all; though if they are all honest and able, each one will give his part.

Now when Christ gave His great commission, He didn't indicate exactly how it was to be carried out. He gave it to the group of disciples who met with Him after His resurrection, and it seems clear that He expected each one to feel his responsibility to witness for his Lord. Yet from the beginning the Church as a body looked upon the extension of the work as a part of its corporate responsibility. So Philip preached first in Samaria on his own initiative; but the church sent its representatives to confirm and establish the work. In Antioch the Spirit had already called Barnabas and Saul to missionary service; but the church was told to send them forth, and they reported to it on their return.

As Christians, we all have been given a great task to perform by our Lord and Saviour. So long as that task has not been completed, it is a lien against each one of us for which He may hold us personally accountable. Yet it is also a lien against the Church. It is the Church's task; but it is also yours and mine. We are all responsible.

THE CHURCH'S RESPONSIBILITY

In speaking of the church's responsibility, we are thinking particularly of the local congregation. Under present conditions of missionary work, the local church, whether it is denominational or not, has certain rather definite obligations to fulfill.

It is just here that a very basic weakness in the missionary enterprise shows up. It is that the local church often is not aware of any such missionary obligations. Or if it is aware of such obligations it chooses to give them very little attention.

In the denominational church a quota may be assigned for the support of missions of that denomination. But small as the quota may be, it often is not met. In the independent church there is no official mission board to assign a quota. So the individual congregation may choose to do something about missions or not, just as it sees fit.

In either case, what the church does will depend largely on its leadership. It is characteristic of American Protestant churches that their affairs are generally managed by a handful of people. This is true even where they are most democratically organized. The average church member seldom does more than attend some of the church services and make a small contribution. Only an inspiring and constructive leadership can get him to take a larger share in the church's business.

But church leaders are not often well informed in missionary matters. Neither do they have much of an interest in affairs that are not under their own control. The pastor himself has usually had little training in the line of missions, even in those of his own denomination. They don't usually present it to him in the seminary as a part of his essential ministry. It is one of the extras, something you can engage in after the local needs are fully met. Even the Ladies' Missionary Society is often busy with other things besides missions because it doesn't have strong missionary leadership.

Yet the world mission of witnessing to Christ among all people is the one great charge that the Saviour gave to His Church after His ascension. The Church really exists for just two purposes: witnessing and fellowship. And all too often we forget the first.

Let us present here four definite responsibilities that pertain to the local church.

First is the responsibility to recognize that missions is a part of the church's essential ministry. It is not a question of whether we should have home missions or foreign missions. That doesn't enter into it. Instead, it is a question of whether the church is going to minister to its own little group or extend its ministry to those who are outside. It is a question of a self-centered ministry or a ministry that looks beyond self to the needs of others.

We don't need to worry about the artificial distinction between home missions and foreign missions. The church that feels keenly the need to reach out and minister to lost souls in its own community can never stop there. A compassionate interest in others isn't even stopped by national boundaries. Once we turn our look outward, "the field is the world."

The same thing is true about the church that is deeply concerned for foreign missions. It can't be blind to the needs on its own doorstep. That is, if it really is concerned for the souls of men and is not merely attracted to missions by the romance of strange lands and people.

This first responsibility is basic. It is the acknowledgment that the church doesn't exist for itself. It is not a social club. It is not a haven of rest. If it is to fulfill its divine purpose it must be missionary. And the first step in fulfilling that purpose is to acknowledge it—to look at it as a duty that must be carried out.

Now when a church recognizes that missions is a part of its essential ministry, it is then responsible to give to missions the same careful, prayerful attention that it gives to any other part of its work. It shouldn't relegate missions to some missionary society within the church as if it didn't concern the whole body of believers. It should plan for missions. It should bring missionary problems to the church prayer meeting and to the governing board. It should give missions a definite place in the church budget.

Too many churches don't have any definite missionary program, even where they are "missionary-minded." One such church comes to mind, which often opened its doors to missionary speakers. The church always made a generous donation to every missionary speaker, *at the time he spoke*. But in the several years of my acquaintance with it, the church never took on the *regular* support of any missionary or mission work. Under such circumstances missions comes to be looked at not as a responsibility but as a pleasurable pastime.

We need to get down to business in missions. Our churches need to stop dabbling and start working. Only so can we meet our God-given responsibility.

Perhaps we ought to say another word about praying for missions. "Prayerful attention" means more than just praying about how much to give. It means more than praying, "God bless the missionaries." It means praying for the work that is going on. It means praying for those who do the work. It means having such a real concern for it all that our concern will express itself in intercessory prayer.

We don't need to go into the values of intercessory prayer. It is enough to know that missionaries themselves count heavily on it. They know that their work alone can never accomplish its purpose. God must work. They know, too, that God is not reluctant to hear their requests. But they know at the same time that God wants church and missionaries to be united in this task. In prayer they can express some of that spiritual union.

The third responsibility of the local church is one that most people think of first. Unfortunately too many of them seem to think it is the only responsibility. It is the task of providing money and other material support for missions. It is an important task, but in carrying it out there are several errors that ought to be avoided.

First, spend the Lord's money for missions as carefully as you would for redecorating the church or for a new church organ. Many a church pays less attention to the distributing of its missionary funds than it does to the choice of a new hymnal. The church should know as much about the causes for which its missionary money goes as if each member were investing his personal funds. We should never be less careful of the Lord's money than of our own.

Second, don't give only for the support of individual missionaries or special projects. It is good to have personal contact with individual missionaries, especially if they have come from your church. It is good, also, to have at least a share in their personal support. The same thing is true of special projects, which do have a way of stimulating people to give. But don't stop there.

The reason is this. Who is going to pay the many other expenses of carrying on the work? Who will pay for the house the missionary lives in? Who will provide him with the literature and other supplies he needs? Who will pay for his travel, or even for the cost of getting his salary to him at his remote post? Who will pay for the scores of other expenses that are necessary for the carrying on of this mission? Don't forget these needs.

Third, when you do support a missionary, don't feel that your support entitles you to dictate his private life. Support him because you believe he is a faithful representative of the Lord, and do it as unto the Lord. Your stewardship ended when you gave the gift; his began. He is responsible to the Lord, not to you, for using the money wisely. Just as you were responsible to the Lord while it was in your hands.

Finally, a fourth and very important responsibility of the

local church to missions is the provision of missionary candidates. Missionaries must come from the local churches. Actually, missionary work in a foreign land is to a large degree a reflection of the spiritual life of the churches at home. To a large degree, we say, but not entirely. It sometimes happens that our missionaries got their deepest spiritual impressions away from the home church. It may have been in a Bible camp, a Christian youth group, a campus Christian organization, or in a Bible training school. But in a general way our foreign missions reflect our Christianity at home.

For this reason it is important for the local church to have a definite program of missionary education. In many of our churches there are untapped resources of manpower for the mission fields, simply because the young people know nothing of the work, have never been faced with the challenge of missions. It is the church's business to challenge them, to turn their hearts in that direction.

CHAPTER IX

THE CHRISTIAN'S RESPONSIBILITY— THE MISSIONARY CALL

As a member of the local church, every Christian has a share in the responsibilities of the church to missions. But there are some other responsibilities that are purely individual. In fact, each individual's participation in the missionary program of the church will depend on his personal response to the appeal of Christ.

The Christian's greatest responsibility is to do just what Saul did on the way to Damascus, to say, "Lord, what wilt thou have me to do?" Until you take this step, it is useless to talk about any other. You can't ease a troubled conscience by offering to support a representative on the mission field if you ought to be there yourself. If you are not surrendered to go to the mission field for Christ, you are not surrendered to Christ!

But only a small part of those who do surrender will actually be sent. Not every volunteer is acceptable for this work. The requirements of missionary service are such that many of those who are willing to go will have to be ruled out. Still, it is the ones who have such a willing heart that Christ can use in every kind of Christian work. Many of our most effective Christian workers at home are those who once wanted to go out as missionaries but were prevented.

This brings up the matter of the missionary call.

THE MISSIONARY CALL

When a young person asks about the missionary call, he usually means, "How can I tell whether the Lord wants *me* on the foreign mission field?"

He may have some interest in Scriptural and philosophic definitions of a call, but it is the answer to this question that he really wants. It is this answer that concerns him, his life and his actions. He will listen patiently to our generalizations if we can make him see just how they apply to his particular case. Otherwise he will turn away in disappointment and perhaps wonder if we really know the answer. Or he may wonder if there is any such thing as being sure of the Lord's will in the matter.

Perhaps his wondering is fully justified. I have heard explanations of the missionary call, and read others, that impressed me as being rationalizations. They seemed to be attempts to provide some sort of doctrinal basis for a course of action already taken, whose real explanation was only vaguely understood.

Sometimes the one doing the explaining has a fixed idea of what the missionary call ought to be. Then in the light of that idea he tries to view his own actions as a fulfillment of the call. He may have an uncomfortable feeling that his own call has not conformed to the set pattern. Yet he hesitates to acknowledge it, even to himself. After all, it is not an easy matter to analyze our own experience in retrospect and avoid reading into it some of the things we think should have been there.

There are other explanations of the call that, while they do touch certain important aspects, usually leave the young Christian still unsatisfied. "A need; a consciousness of that need; and an ability to fill the need" is perhaps as good a definition as one can put in so few words. Yet it seems to imply that human need alone is the call. It leaves out the Lord himself and His relation to the one who is called.

Neither does it provide any basis for deciding which of many needs at home and abroad should have the prior claim. Even if we say, "Go where the need is greatest," the matter is still uncertain. Can we measure need just by the number of needy people? Are the savages of New Guinea more needy than the cultured Japanese? Are *all* foreign fields more needy than *any* home field?

Perhaps what we have to say may not succeed better than others in clarifying the matter. Yet it is a sincere attempt to treat the matter objectively, keeping in view the authority and the teachings of the Scriptures while acknowledging the validity and the value of Christian experience.

Before we can give a clear answer to the question, "What is the missionary call?" there are some false ideas obstructing the way that we must remove. We don't know how some of these ideas began, but they have been repeated so often and are so little challenged that people accept them almost as if they were axiomatic.

First is the idea that we must have some *special* divine call to go beyond the borders of our own country as Christ's witnesses to the lost. That is, we may hear Christ's call to devote our life to Christian service, and so long as we don't leave the limits of the United States we may labor anywhere from Maine to California just as we see the need and find the opportunity. But let someone suggest to us that there is an even greater need, and perhaps an open door, just beyond the national boundary, and immediately we begin to talk about not having a "call" to foreign missionary service. It is as if we thought the boundaries of the nations were established by God and that a special divine passport must be issued—or rather, that a special divine command must be given, before we dare cross over to the other side with the Gospel. We don't hesitate to move three thousand miles from Miami to Seattle at the invitation of a church; but to go a few hours across to Cuba we must first have a special "call"!

Merely to bring such an idea under scrutiny is to refute it. For where can we find any basis to support it? Certainly not in the Scriptures. The Scriptures present the whole world as the field, with no division into "home" and "foreign" fields. Philip preached the Gospel in Samaria, and the refugees from Jerusalem planted the church in Gentile Antioch, with no thought of waiting for a special call to those regions. The refugees were fleeing from the first wave of persecution, and wherever they went they spoke of the Saviour. The idea of a special divine call to minister beyond the borders of Judea and Galilee does not seem to have entered their heads. They were witnesses to everyone everywhere.

Of course those who first established the church in Antioch were not what we would call today "full-time" workers. It may be well to look at those who took the leadership there later and gave full time to a Christian ministry.

First mentioned is Barnabas, who already had some prominence in the work in Jerusalem. It was the Jerusalem church that sent Barnabas to Antioch. They had heard of the work there and apparently believed that Barnabas would be just the man to look into the situation and establish the new believers in the faith. Barnabas went, found a need for his services, and decided to stay.

But Barnabas saw that another man could be used there, too. He remembered Saul, whom he had first introduced to the believers in Jerusalem and who later had had to go home to Tarsus, in Asia Minor. We don't know what Saul was doing at the time, but Tarsus was not too far from Antioch. So Barnabas went there to get Saul and bring him to help out in the new church.

We may well assume that both Barnabas and Saul waited on the Lord before agreeing to go to Antioch. But it is perfectly clear, and the Scriptures plainly state, that the initiative in both instances came from other men. The Jerusalem church "sent" Barnabas, and Barnabas "brought" Saul. Not a word, not even a hint is given that any special divine call, any unusual spiritual experience was needed to overcome their reluctance to leave their own land as ministers of Christ. True, Barnabas was a native of Cyprus and Saul of Cilicia, but Antioch was still a foreign field to them both.

As for the other "prophets and teachers" in Antioch, "Simeon that was called Niger, and Lucius of Cyrene, and Manaen, which had been brought up with Herod the tetrarch," it is evident that at least Lucius and Manaen were not from Antioch and so could be called foreign missionaries. But there is no indication of the way in which they had come into the work there. They may have been among the refugees. Or they may have been among the prophets mentioned in Acts 11:27 who came down from Jerusalem at the same time as Agabus. At any rate, the fact that they were ministering in a foreign field didn't call for any special comment.

In all the New Testament account, there is only one instance when a national or geographic boundary seemed to require a *special* call before the missionaries would decide to pass it. That was on Paul's second missionary journey, when he and his companions reached Troas. There they got a remarkable revelation of God's will that they should go on over into Europe.

This unusual experience, generally named the "Macedonian call," is often held to be the typical missionary call. Even some otherwise careful missionary writers and speakers have plainly called it such. They have tried to show how it applies to the situation young Christians face today, when they are confronted with the challenge of foreign missionary service. They encourage young people to look for some such experience as Paul had there at Troas, before applying for missionary service. And when the experience does not come, the young people are confused and discouraged.

This is really the second of the false ideas that keeps us from a proper understanding of the missionary call. We need to realize that *the "Macedonian call" was positively not the missionary call!* It wasn't even a typical call of any sort! It was an unusual experience, and all the more striking because it was so unusual. Perhaps it had to be striking to accomplish its purpose at that time and in the hearts of those men.

It is not at all unreasonable to suppose that on other occasions, even today, God may make use of such unusual means to call men to one task or another. Yet in the New Testament this case was the exception rather than the rule. And in Christian experience today such occurrences are still exceptional.

We have said that the "Macedonian call" was not the missionary call. Even a superficial reading of the preceding chapters in the Acts should make this abundantly clear. Paul was already a missionary; he had been a missionary for some years. Actually this incident took place in the midst of his second great missionary tour. He was already in a foreign land when the vision came. And it came, not to call him and his companions to missionary service, but to call them to extend their operations beyond Asia Minor to Europe. If we can remove from our thinking the idea that this was a typical call to foreign missionary service, we shall clear the way for a better understanding of what such a call really is.

A third misunderstanding that needs to be cleared up is the notion that the missionary call *necessarily* is associated with some definite field. Some young people are greatly perturbed because, while they are sure that the Lord wants them to go forth as foreign missionaries, they find it difficult to know precisely to what field they should go. Here again the common idea is inconsistent with the Scriptural examples.

When Barnabas and Saul started out on their first missionary journey together, they knew the work they were to do, for the Spirit had said to the church, "Separate me Barnabas and Saul for *the work whereunto I have called them.*" But it is doubtful that they knew just in what places they were to carry on this work. Note carefully their itinerary. Cyprus was nearby, it was unevangelized, and it was the homeland of Barnabas. So it was natural that they should go there first. From western Cyprus the next logical step was the mainland of Asia Minor. Here the evangelization continued until they reached the border of Paul's own province of Cilicia. Presumably he had carried on work there before going to Antioch. To establish better the work they had done, they now retraced their steps and finally returned to Antioch with their mission completed. Maybe the trip had been planned ahead of time, but various details, such as Mark's leaving them when they entered Asia Minor, seem to show otherwise.

But whether or not they knew just where they were going on that first trip, Paul certainly didn't know in advance the itinerary of his second journey. He started out to revisit the churches they had established before. But soon he was trying other doors. Finding some of them temporarily closed, he pushed on in the only forward direction that was open, until he reached Troas. From there, the Macedonian vision gave him a clear enough call to the next place. But Macedonia was only a stepping-stone, for without any other vision Paul moved on westward and southward into Greece until he came to the city of Corinth.

On the return from Corinth, Paul visited the province of Asia. The Lord had forbidden him to preach there earlier on this same tour. He spent only a brief time there in the city of Ephesus, but later on he returned for a much more extended ministry.

Paul's great trip to Rome was not the result of any vision or special revelation. In writing to the brethren there before he went, he said that he had desired for many years to make the trip and see them. Since his apostolic ministry had now been completed where he was, he would soon be ready to visit Rome on his way to Spain (Rom. 15:23).

So, as we review the career of the great missionary to the Gentiles, we see that he seldom enjoyed a special revelation to direct his movements. Only twice after his conversion do we hear of such an experience. Once was when the Lord told him to leave Jerusalem, since his mission was to be to the Gentiles

(Acts 22:17–21). He was told to leave but wasn't told where to go. The other occasion was when he received the Macedonian vision. Here only the important initial step was revealed. In fact, he had only two alternatives—either to go on across to Europe or to go back along the road he had come. It was not a question of choice of field but a question of advance or consolidation. And the Lord directed advance.

To sum up: (1) a *special* divine call is not necessary to witness for Christ beyond the national border; (2) the striking vision that Paul received at Troas, the so-called "Macedonian call," was *not* his missionary call, nor is it typical of such a call; and (3) the call to missionary service is not *necessarily* associated with a definite field at home or abroad.

It might seem from this that we have completely ruled out the idea of a call. But this is not so. We have merely tried to clear the ground in order to construct a more Scriptural and sound doctrine of the missionary call. The call is not lacking, in fact it is fundamental. No one should go to any mission field without a sense of call if he expects to enjoy God's blessing on his ministry. But to wait or look for an experience that at best is quite unusual is to open the way for disappointment and frustration.

There are two aspects of the missionary call, one general and one particular. For clearness of thinking we usually do well to distinguish the two. We must recognize also that the first is fundamental to the second.

The general missionary call is synonymous with the "great commission." It is expressed in various ways: "Go ye therefore and teach all nations . . . Go ye into all the world and preach the gospel . . . As my Father hath sent me, even so send I you . . . Ye shall be witnesses unto me . . . unto the uttermost parts of the earth." But the message is the same. It is the call of Christ to those who follow Him to go out and witness for Him everywhere. It includes all of His disciples; not one is omitted from its scope. The Christian who fails to bear witness to his Saviour is disobedient to this call, which is meant for him.

This call is general because it includes all Christians as prospective missionaries. But it is general also because it includes all unbelievers as the missionary field. It is not a question of home missions or foreign missions, of city missions or missions on the frontier. This is a call to be Christ's ambassadors to lost sinners without regard to the places where they may be found.

There is no use trying to talk about a special call to the foreign mission field until the matter of this general missionary call is settled. It is just as useless as it would be to discuss the call to missionary service before the issue of putting one's faith in the Saviour has been settled. It has been well said that a trip across the ocean doesn't make a missionary. But neither does failure to go abroad keep a man from being a missionary.

Lest you should be tempted to discount the importance of this general missionary call, take time to observe how similar it is to your call to salvation. In fact, if you look carefully through the New Testament you will find that the word "call" is most often used in connection with salvation rather than with service.

Note that the call to salvation is a general call issued to all sinners. It is a call to "whosoever will." Occasionally the Lord speaks to an individual and says, "Follow me"; but usually His invitation is "Come unto me *all* ye that labor and are heavy laden." Wasn't that the kind of call you answered when you came to Christ to receive His salvation? Wasn't it a general invitation you accepted, but one that you realized was sincerely intended to include you? Did you wait for a special divine invitation, an audible voice to call out your name? Did you wait to be drafted?

Clearly the general call to salvation is enough when the sinner hears it and realizes it is meant for him. But the call is not complete, is not effectual, until the sinner responds,

"Lord, I believe!" In the same way the general call to witness for Christ is enough when the believer hears it and realizes that it is meant for him. But to make it effectual he too must say, "Here am I, Lord; send me!" When God calls and man responds, then the divine call is complete.

Actually, for foreign missionary service as for any other, it is not *essential* to have any other call than this general call. Christ's missionaries are those who have a deep and compelling sense of their obligation to obey His command and make known His salvation to all men.

Many missionaries are mentioned in the New Testament besides the apostles, some by name, as Titus and Apollos and Epaphras; and others anonymously, as the Thessalonian believers. But so far as we have information, the majority carried on their ministry in obedience to this general call. With the living Christ in their hearts, they were constrained to be His witnesses everywhere.

Still, there is an individual aspect to the call, and in some cases a separate individual call. We have spoken of the response to Christ's general commission. This of course is an individual response. No one can answer for another, not even a father for his son, much as he may want to. It is in this response that we see clearly the hand of the Holy Spirit. He who opens the eyes of sinners to behold the Saviour and moves them to accept His invitation to receive life in Him, is the same one who illumines the understanding of the saints and opens their ears to the call to make the Saviour known in every land. The way in which He does this we may understand as little in the one case as in the other, but it is just as effectual. "Whereas I was blind, now I see," may be all the testimony we can give. But it is enough.

It is in this individual aspect of the missionary call that we run into the question of fields of service. Shall it be the foreign field or the home field? If the foreign field, which one? Such questions are constantly asked and should be answered.

Hardly ever are they answered with a vision or some other such striking experience. But we shouldn't think that this is impossible. Still the normal way is otherwise.

In this matter friends may counsel and preachers exhort, and missionary speakers may even resort to scolding. But the final decision is between you and God. Sometimes, in order to see the matter in its proper relationships, we might do well to drop the word "call" and speak of this as a matter of guidance. There may be a special call, but more often the young Christian is simply waiting to be shown *where* he is to serve.

The general principles of guidance certainly apply here: a recognition of the need of guidance, a willingness to be led, a deliberate renunciation of self-interest, a close walk with God so as to be sensitive to His wishes, as well as a constant use of the Word of God and earnest prayer.

Christ's own command to "look on the fields" should lead us to contemplate their needs and feel the compassion that such needs should inspire. A careful study of the fields, such as William Carey made, may open the way for God's guidance. Listening to missionaries from various fields is helpful. At first it may seem confusing, because of the vastness of the task and the needs. But after a time it often happens that one of those fields begins to stand out in your consciousness as the place where God can use you to the greatest advantage.

Consider carefully the question whether you should serve Christ in the home country or on some foreign field. To think that unless God calls you specially to some foreign land you ought to take up work at home is the worst possible attitude to take. There are too many Christian workers who have drifted into some position in the homeland simply because they have not been called to anything else.

How do you dare to stand in *any* pulpit as a minister of Christ without the clear conviction that He has called you there? The call of the pulpit committee or of the church is no substitute for Christ's call. What makes you think that it is any less necessary to feel an overpowering divine compulsion to give your life to a ministry in Middletown, U.S.A., than in a Congo forest? If a call is necessary for the one, it is just as necessary for the other.

Should you serve at home or abroad? Don't expect a satisfactory answer to this question until you have answered first a couple of others. Are you sure God wants you in full-time service for Him? Your answer to this question may mean service on the foreign field; it often does. But perhaps just as often the Lord calls a man to his ministry first, and perhaps even gives him a time of service at home, before He sends him abroad as His messenger to other peoples. At all events it is important to know whether you should be set apart exclusively for Christian service.

Too many of us take it for granted that full consecration necessarily means going into full-time Christian ministry. Such an idea tends in the same direction as the idea held in the Middle Ages that for a really devout life one had to withdraw from the world and enter some monastery. It may take out of the workaday world those very elements that are needed to keep it from ever increasing corruption. It fosters the all too commonly held notion that "business and religion don't mix." As a matter of fact, there is no good reason why a laborer or a businessman may not be as earnest a Christian witness and as truly spiritual as any minister. Many are.

But even if you are sure that the Lord wants you in full-time service, there is still another question to be answered. Are you ready to surrender your own will to His and gladly do whatever He wants you to do? Such a surrender is not easy. Neither is it as complete oftentimes as we suppose at the moment. Yet, is it right to expect God to lead you to the field of *His* choice, when you have already determined in your own heart where *you* want to go? If you really want His guidance you have to be ready to put yourself in His hands and gladly follow His directions, wherever He may lead.

Does selfish ambition enter into your plans, the desire for recognition and praise from other Christians? It is better to please God than men; it is even more satisfying to your own soul. Are you afraid of privations, and do you shrink from a venture that means a radical change in your way of living and brings you into contact with strange, unfamiliar people and circumstances? Your Saviour himself has promised to be with you all the days until the end—*if you go!* That promise is connected with the command to go!

On the other hand, there are some for whom other fields always appear greener than those close at home. There is for some a purely human attraction in strange lands and people. They need to ask themselves, "Can I be happy to stay at home and minister in an unromantic field, if that is where Christ wants me most?" For some the decision to stay is fully as difficult as for others the decision to go. But the call to stay may be just as definite and the results of obedience just as joyful.

Now if you have answered these two preliminary questions in the affirmative, if you are sure the Lord wants you to dedicate your whole life to His service and are confident that your greatest desire is to fulfill His will, whatever that will may be and wherever it may lead, the main question becomes much easier to answer. Not that anyone can answer it for you. You should not accept their answers even when they urge them on you. This is between you and God. It is He who must guide you.

But it may be of help to know how at times He has led others. If the testimonies of those who have experienced *salvation* are honored of the Lord in leading others to an enjoyment of that same experience, then the testimonies of those whom the Lord has called and blessed in *missionary service* may be used in revealing God's ways of guidance to other puzzled young Christians.

We shall give some of these testimonies in the next chapter.

CHAPTER X

THE MISSIONARY CALL— TESTIMONIES

WE WISH WE KNEW about the missionary calls of all of our great missionaries. It would help us to see more clearly the many ways in which the Lord leads men into missionary work. But we don't. Only now and then do we get a clear picture of how the Lord dealt with one of them. Sometimes we have it in his own words. Sometimes we have to depend on the accuracy of his biographer.

In this chapter we are going to talk about seven great missionaries. They all lived in the past century, so their works have stood the test of time. Four of them were British and three were American. (The day had not yet come when American missionaries outnumbered all others.) They went to several fields in Africa and the Orient. And the information we have about their calls is fairly clear. We shall give their own words when we can.

DAVID LIVINGSTONE

The very name Livingstone spells Africa. No missionary is better known today. Very few ever captured the imagination of their own day to such an extent.

Yet Livingstone did not at first intend to go to Africa. In fact, he didn't plan to be a missionary at all. Not that he was opposed to missions. He thought every Christian ought to be a soul-winner. It ought to be his chief desire and aim. But when it came to foreign missions, Livingstone's idea was that he would give money for it. He would give everything he earned above what he needed to live.

But that wasn't God's idea. One day Livingstone read an item that changed his whole purpose. Dr. Karl Gützlaff, brilliant and devout missionary pioneer, had traveled up and down the coasts of East Asia all the way from Siam to Korea. Now he was pleading for missionaries for the great empire of China. And when Livingstone thought on those millions of Chinese without Christ, and on the lack of suitable workers to give them the Gospel, he decided to prepare and offer himself.

For China, did we say? Then how did he get to Africa? The Opium War did it. Livingstone prepared to be a medical missionary in China, and the London Missionary Society accepted him. But before he could sail, the war closed the door. Now what should he do? They suggested the West Indies. But he didn't think his medical training would be so useful there.

At this point Robert Moffat entered the picture. The great South Africa missionary was at home in Britain speaking about the work in that dark land.

> I had occasion to call for someone at Mrs. Sewell's, a boarding-house for young missionaries in Aldersgate street, where Livingstone lived. I observed soon that this young man was interested in my story, that he would sometimes come quietly and ask me a question or two, and that he was always desirous to know where I was to speak in public, and attended on these occasions.
>
> By-and-by he asked me whether he would do for Africa. I said I believed he would, if he would not go to an old station, but would advance to unoccupied ground, specifying the vast plain to the north, where I had sometimes seen, in the morning sun, the smoke of a thousand villages, where no missionary had ever been.
>
> At last Livingstone said, "What is the use of my waiting

for the end of this abominable Opium War? I will go at once to Africa!" The Directors concurred, and Africa became his sphere.

JOHN G. PATON

When an author wants to write a thrilling missionary story for young people, he is very likely to turn to the life of John G. Paton. Not many can compare with it. Paton went to work among cannibals in the New Hebrides islands of the South Pacific. He lived a long life and an exciting one. And he found the time to tell about it.

Paton began as a city missionary in his native Scotland. He seemed to be doing well, but he says:

> Happy in my work as I felt, and successful by the blessing of God, yet I continually heard, and chiefly during my last years in the Divinity Hall, the wail of the perishing Heathen in the South Seas; and I saw that few were caring for them, while I well knew that many would be ready to take up my work in Calton and carry it forward perhaps with more efficiency than myself.
>
> Without revealing the state of my mind to any person, this was the supreme subject of my daily meditation and prayer; and this also led me to enter upon those medical studies, in which I purposed taking the full course; but at the close of my third year, an incident occurred, which led me at once to offer myself for the Foreign Mission field.
>
> The Reformed Presbyterian Church of Scotland, in which I had been brought up, had been advertising for another Missionary to join the Rev. John Inglis in his grand work in the New Hebrides. Dr. Bates, the excellent convener of the Heathen Missions Committee, was deeply grieved, because for two years their appeal had failed.
>
> At length, the Synod, after much prayer and consultation, felt the claims of the Heathen so urgently pressed upon them by the Lord's repeated calls, that they resolved to cast lots, to discover whether God would thus select any

Minister to be relieved from his home-charge, and designated as a Missionary to the South Seas. Each member of
the Synod, as I was informed, agreed to hand in, after
solemn appeal to God, the names of the three best qualified in his esteem for such a work, and he who had the clear
majority was to be loosed from his congregation, and to
proceed to the Mission field—or the first and second highest, if two could be secured.

Hearing this debate, and feeling an intense interest in
these most unusual proceedings, I remember yet the
hushed solemnity of the prayer before the names were
handed in. I remember the strained silence that held the
Assembly while the scrutinizers retired to examine the
papers; and I remember how tears blinded my eyes when
they returned to announce that the result was so indeci-
sive, that it was clear that the Lord had not in that way
provided a missionary. The cause was once again solemnly
laid before God in prayer, and a cloud of sadness appeared
to fall over all the Synod.

The Lord kept saying within me, "Since none better
qualified can be got, rise and offer yourself!" Almost overpowering was the impulse to answer aloud, "Here am I,
send me!" But I was dreadfully afraid of mistaking my
own emotions for the will of God.

So I resolved to make it a subject of close deliberation
and prayer for a few days longer, and to look at the pro-
posal from every possible aspect.

From every aspect at which I could look the whole facts
in the face, the voice within me sounded like a voice from
God.

James Chalmers

"Tamate," the natives called him. "The Great Heart of
New Guinea," said Robert Louis Stevenson. And certainly no
one had a wilder field, nor one that called for a greater heart.
His first ten years in the islands farther east were tame in comparison with the years on the southeast coast of New Guinea.

He lived continually in the shadow of death. A man's man. And, unlike Paton, he was finally killed and eaten by the cannibals.

Chalmers says that it was in his teens that he came to the great decision of his life:

> I remember it well. Our Sunday school class had been held in the vestry as usual. The lesson was finished, and we had marched back into the chapel to sing, answer questions, and to listen to a short address.
>
> I was sitting at the head of the seat, and can even now see Mr. Meikle taking from his breast-pocket a copy of the *United Presbyterian Record,* and hear him say that he was going to read an interesting letter to us from a missionary in Fiji.
>
> The letter was read. It spoke of cannibalism, and of the power of the Gospel, and at the close of the reading, looking over his spectacles, and with wet eyes, he said, "I wonder if there is a boy here this afternoon who will yet become a missionary, and by-and-by bring the Gospel to cannibals?" And the response of my heart was, "Yes, God helping me, and I will."

The unusual thing about Chalmers' call was that it came, as he says, several years before his conversion. He forgot his decision for a time and wandered far from Christ. Then came his conversion, his preparation for the ministry, and his city missionary work in Glasgow. He remembered his youthful vow, and after several talks with Dr. Turner of Samoa he applied to be sent to the South Pacific.

ADONIRAM JUDSON

Every American Baptist knows Judson's name. Not only was he one of the first party of missionaries to go out from the United States, but he later inspired the beginning of what is now the American Baptist Foreign Mission Society. Burma was his field. He could scarcely have hit upon a harder one. Yet he came to be called "the Apostle of Burma."

According to his son, two things moved Judson to go to the mission field. After his striking conversion, he had entered Andover Seminary to prepare for the ministry. There he came in touch with Samuel Mills and other missionary-minded students. They were just a small group, but deadly in earnest. And Judson soon became as zealous as the others for the starting of an American mission society.

But it was not only the fellowship with these other students. It was also a sermon. He had already finished his first year at the seminary when he read it. The sermon had been preached in England by Dr. Claudius Buchanan, a chaplain of the British East India Company. It had for its title "The Star in the East" and spoke of the power and progress of the Gospel in India. Judson's son says that "this sermon fell like a spark into the tinder of Judson's soul." Six months later he made his final decision to serve Christ as a foreign missionary.

John Scudder

John Scudder was the first American medical missionary to India. He went out under the earliest American society, the American Board of Commissioners for Foreign Missions. But he later opened the Arcot field of the Reformed Church in America. He was also the head of one of the most remarkable missionary families in history, whose members through half a dozen generations have served as missionaries on many fields.

Scudder wanted to be a minister. But when his father strongly opposed the idea, he turned to medicine. In this field he did such good work that he soon built up a good practice and began to prosper financially. Then one day the course of his life was suddenly changed.

In the course of his practice he went to attend a Christian woman who was ill. In her room he saw a tract, *The Conversion of the World, or the Claims of Six Hundred Millions.* He became interested and asked to borrow it. At home he read it over and over, until finally he fell to his knees saying, "Lord, what wilt thou have me to do?" He didn't hear an audible voice, but in his heart he knew the answer was, "Go and preach the gospel to the heathen."

But Scudder couldn't make the final decision alone. He had a wife to think of. He said to himself, "I have one to consult whose interests are blended with my own, and whose happiness may be seriously affected by my decision. I will lay the subject before *her* mind as it lies before mine. If she say nay, I shall regard it as settling the question of duty."

"From love to Christ," he added, "and a sense of duty, she decided for the life of a missionary. That purpose never gave way. It never even faltered."

At about that time the American Board advertised for a doctor who would be willing to go as a missionary. Dr. Scudder applied and was sent out.

JAMES M. THOBURN

James M. Thoburn, later Bishop Thoburn of the Methodist Episcopal Church in India, was one of the most illustrious missionaries of that church. No one ever did more to promote the expansion of his church in the Indian peninsula. And his efforts extended beyond India itself to other lands.

From shortly after his conversion, Thoburn says that he was repeatedly faced with the challenge of the mission field. He became a minister and was appointed to a circuit of churches. Then one day, after he had preached for about a year, the challenge came again with increased force. He had sat down to read his church paper and was struck by the leading editorial. It was an appeal for six young men to go to India. He writes:

> I was powerfully moved by the appeal, not so much by anything it contained as by a strong impression that I ought to be one of the six young men to go forth. I

dropped the paper and fell upon my knees and promised God that I would accept the call if only He would make it clear that He was sending me. I asked for some token, for some definite indication that I was called from above, not only in a general way to become a missionary, but to that special field and at that special time.

Thoburn made up his mind to ask the advice of his presiding elder as soon as he saw him. When they met, the elder, not knowing what was on the young preacher's mind, remarked, "I met Bishop Janes on the train this morning."

"Bishop Janes!" Thoburn replied. "What can he be doing out here?"

"He is on his way west, looking for missionaries for India. He wants six immediately."

Thoburn's heart leaped into his throat. But before he could reply, the elder continued, "James, how would you like to go?"

"It is very singular," the young preacher replied, "but I have come here with the special purpose of asking your advice about going to India."

"Well, I must tell you that you have been in my mind all morning. I incline to think you ought to go. I have felt so ever since the bishop told me his errand."

Going to a little "prophet-chamber," Thoburn prayed for guidance. He says:

> I did not receive any message, or realize any new conviction, or come down from my sacred audience with God feeling that the matter was forever settled, and yet that hour stands out in my life as the burning bush must have stood in the memory of Moses. It was my burning bush. It has followed me through all the years which have passed.

Alexander M. Mackay

It was once said that Uganda was "the brightest spot on the map of Africa." The man who first sowed the Gospel in that central African kingdom was Alexander Mackay, of the Church Missionary Society. He did not live to see the great harvest, but few tales of dauntless courage and persistence are more inspiring than his life.

Mackay prepared himself to become a civil engineer. Missions was not in his mind when he left Britain for Germany to continue his studies. But he was a sincere Christian, so he was not deaf to the Lord's call when it came. And it came in a most unusual way. In a letter to his sister from Berlin he wrote:

> Well, it is through you, or what you wrote me on December 11 last, that what I now have to write you exists.
>
> You told me then that you had been at a social meeting of our Literary Association in Chalmers Memorial Church; that there you heard Dr. Burns Thomson . . . urge young men of the Association to give themselves to the work and go out as medical missionaries . . . to Madagascar . . .
>
> Well, I am not a doctor, and therefore cannot go as such; but I am an engineer, and propose, if the Lord will, to go as an engineering missionary. Miserable chimera you will no doubt call such an idea. Yet immediately on the receipt of your letter I wrote Dr. Bonar, offering myself to such work, and asking his advice.

A couple of months later he wrote to his father:

> Man is a volent being, by virtue of what God has made him. Yet man is inwardly swayed by external circumstances.
>
> Now if to my ears or hands there comes the message, "Who will go to preach the gospel in Madagascar?" how can I, except in unbelief, say otherwise than that God caused that message to come to me? And if it is of God, must I not say, "Here am I; send me"?

The London Missionary Society was not able to use Mackay in Madagascar at the time, but in 1875 the Church Missionary

Society appealed for a worker of Mackay's qualifications for East Africa near Mombasa. He saw the appeal and wrote home,

> Remembering that Duff first thought of Africa as a mission field, but was sent to India, and that Livingstone originally intended to evangelize China, but the Lord willed he should spend his life in Africa, so perhaps the Lord means me, after all, to turn my attention to the Dark Continent; accordingly I have offered my services to the C.M.S.—the greatest missionary society in the world—for Mombasa.

The C.M.S., however, had already engaged another man. But a little later there appeared in the *Daily Telegraph* Stanley's letter describing his visit to Mtesa, king of Uganda, and challenging Christendom to send missionaries to that land. The C.M.S. took up the challenge and accepted Mackay for the work.

SUMMARY

These, then, were the missionary calls of seven really great missionaries of Christ. No one would question that they were truly called, though the circumstances of their calling were so different from one another. In fact, one great lesson that we can learn from their testimonies is the diversity of ways in which God may lead.

Notice well the following facts. Not one of these missionaries saw a vision, dreamed a dream, or heard an audible voice calling him to go. All of them were influenced by reading or hearing an appeal for willing workers. Yet the appeal was general. Only Thoburn had a personal appeal made to him, and it was just one of the confirmations of his call.

But most of these men were in places where they could readily hear the call when it came. Paton, Thoburn and Chalmers were ministering at home. Judson was studying for the ministry, and Scudder had wanted to do so. Judson was also influenced by missionary-minded companions.

In six cases the call had some connection with a definite field. Yet only three actually served in those fields. The others went to different places.

From this we can see that the missionary call is not likely to come in a miraculous way. Neither does it come to all people in the same way. Rather, if we wanted to define it we should probably have to say that *the missionary call is the "great commission," plus the assurance in your heart, no matter how it comes, that God wants* you *as His witness abroad.*

CHAPTER XI

MISSIONARY QUALIFICATIONS—
ESSENTIAL

W E SAID that the individual Christian's first responsibility to missions is to offer himself. However, we added that the requirements for foreign service are such as to rule out a great many who would like to serve as missionaries. They just wouldn't be able to qualify. In this chapter and the next we shall talk about missionary qualifications.

Just what qualifications are needed in the foreign missionary? In general, we may say, all the qualifications that make a good witness for Christ in the homeland, plus some others. These others are made necessary because he does his witnessing in a foreign land, under unfavorable circumstances, and with a broader field of operations.

The requirements of an ambassador for Christ in a foreign land are very high, and we would do wrong to minimize them. He must perform his ministry in unfamiliar surroundings. He does it through a new language or languages that he has to learn by dint of hard work. He labors among peoples who are often hostile, and whose culture is quite different from his own. His message is open to suspicion, since he is a foreigner. As often as not, he finds that the climate and the living conditions hamper his work and sap his strength. Yet he has to carry on a broad ministry, and that with only a fraction of the equipment and helps that are available in the homeland.

Whatever the mission *boards* may require, the mission *field* demands men and women of the highest caliber and exacts the utmost from them.

Contrary to what many think, Christian piety alone is not enough for missionary service. Missionaries are not dreamy-eyed idealists, as the cartoonists picture them. By force of circumstance they have to be realists. They couldn't last long otherwise. Their work makes demands upon every faculty and most of the knowledge they possess, even among primitive peoples.

Yet the most essential qualifications for a good missionary are spiritual. There are others that are valuable, but the spiritual ones are basic. The ten we are going to discuss may not be exhaustive, but they are characteristics that mark every successful missionary of Christ. Do you have them?

(1) *Devotion.* Whole-hearted devotion to Christ and His Gospel is a prime requisite. You can't do without it and be a missionary. You can't win others to Christ if your own allegiance is shaky. If you are uncertain about your faith, if you can't say with heartfelt assurance, "I *know* whom I have believed," you had better stay at home. Missionaries are those who are thoroughly "sold" on their faith.

(2) *Spirituality.* The missionary of Christ must be spiritually-minded, as opposed to material-mindedness. That is because his chief aims are spiritual. You don't reach spiritual ends by physical means. The missionary can't disregard the physical; it is a necessary part of his life and work. But he dare not let it take the first place. Yet the temptations on the field are as great as at home, if not actually greater, to regard material things too highly. It is not easy, even for a missionary, to "seek first the kingdom of God and his righteousness," but it is necessary. The eternal value of the soul—of the things of the spirit—must occupy first place in the mind of Christ's messenger to the heathen.

(3) *Trust.* Some missionaries are called "faith" mission-

aries. But they are not the only ones who live a life of faith. On the foreign field we are usually far from the ordinary means of human help that we are used to. Sometimes funds and supplies fail. Sometimes illness strikes when no doctor or nurse is in ready reach. The authorities may be against us and the people suspicious and unfriendly. The powers of darkness seem overwhelming. Even in our own hearts we struggle with discouragement, and there are no Christian advisers to whom we can turn for comfort and encouragement. We come to realize that in ourselves we can do nothing.

Have you learned to trust God for every need, material and spiritual? You will need to know that lesson to be a missionary. Trust doesn't spring up full-fledged in a time of crisis. You don't get it when you reach the field. Rather, it grows little by little as you look to God for the small things and find Him faithful. And there are plenty of chances to learn to trust Him, even in the life of a student. Then when the time of great need comes, your heart spontaneously turns to the One you know can meet every need.

(4) *Love.* People expect the missionary to be the very embodiment of God's love to man. Isn't he sometimes the only representative of the Christian Gospel in a place? And isn't the heart of that Gospel the love of God? The love of God that sent His Son into the world to die for sinful men is the same love that sends the missionary to make that salvation known.

It is easy to love some people. It is not so easy to love others. But the missionary cannot choose to love just those who are attractive. It is the love of Christ that constrains the missionary to go, the love that poured itself out for all of us when we were His enemies. It is the love of Christ which the missionary aims to reveal as best he can, pouring out his own life in unselfish devotion to the people to whom he goes. He learns to think of them as "my people." Unless he loves them, he can hardly keep going. Unless he loves them, his work is fruitless.

(5) *Moral courage.* There are people whose standards of

right and wrong are very flexible. They can be bent to fit almost any situation so as to offend no one. There are others who believe that "right is right"; but they don't believe it very audibly. That is, they haven't the courage to stand up for what they believe. Both types are "easy to get along with." They never stir up arguments.

But such people don't make good missionaries. Firm standards of right and wrong are essential equipment for the missionary. And not only firm standards, but the courage to make them known. He may be called "narrow-minded." That is part of the price for having convictions. But it is the water in the narrow channel that flows with greatest force.

Not that the missionary needs to be obnoxiously opinionated. We are talking only about right and wrong. Neither does he have to be overly harsh in denouncing sin. The Scripture advises "speaking the truth in love." But the truth must be spoken, sin must be faced frankly and openly, or else he has no ministry worth the name.

(6) *Purpose.* There is an ailment afflicting many young people today that we might call lack of purpose. They are not sure just what they want to do. They don't know at what goal they ought to aim. So they refrain from any choice, just waiting for circumstances to show them what is likely to be most to their advantage.

Now a temporary uncertainty, especially in making a decision that is likely to affect the whole course of your life, is not serious. You want to be careful. But if you always find it hard to make up your mind; if you habitually show a lack of eager purposefulness; if you don't know what it is to have one great aim to which you bring other interests into subjection, then you won't make much of a missionary.

A missionary must be a man of vision. His vision must be a high and worthy objective toward which he dedicates the whole course of his life. He needs a God-given vision.

(7) *Discernment.* In this matter again, the true missionary

is quite different from his caricature. He is a man of vision but not a visionary. His vision may lead him to see beyond present circumstances, but he dare not be blind to things as they are. The very continuance of his work may depend on his discernment. He must be able to see the real issues at stake in the many problems he faces. In plain language, he needs lots of common sense.

(8) *Zeal.* A real missionary is rightly a zealot. His zeal doesn't have to be of that effervescent type that shows itself in vigorous demonstrations of emotion. It may be an intense, slow-burning but all-consuming type that drives him steadily on in spite of opposition. But a zealot he is. A lazy, indifferent missionary just has no place on the field. We can do better without him.

(9) *Constancy.* There are disappointments and discouragements in every field. Perhaps we are more often disappointed with ourselves than with any other one thing. The mission field shows us how weak we really are. And then there comes the temptation to give up.

It's easy to say that if you are sure the Lord sent you there, you won't give up. But there's more to it than that. It's too easy to persuade yourself that you may have been mistaken, or that the Lord may have changed His mind. It's the one who has learned the lesson of constancy who usually holds fast. He has learned to keep on in spite of discouragement. The Lord can depend on him and so can his fellow workers.

You can't enjoy real success without such perseverance. But, like faith, it isn't something you can work up overnight. Instead it is the result of constant practice in dependability: in employment, in studies, in social relationships, in family obligations, etc. Have you come to the place where people can always depend on you?

(10) *Leadership.* Missionary work calls for leaders. Whether they want to or not, those who go out as missionaries have to take places of leadership. Bringing men to Christ is only the

beginning. The missionary then needs to lead them on in their spiritual development. He needs to lead them in the formation of the church. He needs to lead in the training of national workers who will carry on the work. He must break the way in Christian literature and a dozen other lines of work—things that are needed for the full expression and development of the Christian life. So he must have the qualities of leadership—especially initiative and responsibility.

The ten qualifications we have mentioned are essential for good missionary service. Insofar as a missionary is weak in one or another, his work is bound to suffer. They are qualifications that have marked the ministry of the really great missionaries.

But they are extremely hard to measure. How can a mission board tell what amount of each is needed before it sends out a candidate? And can they possibly tell how much he really has? Clearly they are of most use to the candidate himself. He can use them in examining his own heart and life. He can try to strengthen what is weak. Getting by the board is incidental; he wants to be a *missionary!*

CHAPTER XII

MISSIONARY QUALIFICATIONS
(*Continued*)

THE SPIRITUAL QUALIFICATIONS given in the previous chapter are essential for missionary service. But in the very nature of modern missions other requirements must also be met. The requirements differ from mission to mission and from field to field, so all that we can do is explain general principles or trends. You need to find out the demands of any particular mission from the mission itself.

But remember that under some circumstances the mission may make exceptions. Of course the exceptions are only for what it thinks are good reasons and are at its own discretion. The mission, you see, tries to look at the candidate as an individual and not as a mere collection of qualifications. They try to see how he would fit in with their needs and program.

Note, too, that some boards are strict in their requirements, while others are notoriously lax. If you want to have the happiest and most fruitful service, set your aim high.

We begin with the physical requirements because they are the most obvious and the easiest to judge.

First as to age. Naturally no one is too old or too young to witness for Christ. But when we come to choosing a messenger who can go to a foreign land and make known the message of Christ among a strange people, a man who can establish and build up a church there, the question of age is often quite important.

The general principle is this. The candidate needs to be young enough: (1) to learn well the language of the people to whom he goes; (2) to adapt himself physically and mentally to new conditions of living; and (3) to look forward to enough years of ministry to be worth the necessary expense for his equipment, his passage to the field, and the special training the mission will have to give him. On the other hand, he needs to be old enough to be mature in thinking and acting, so he can take on the serious responsibilities of a missionary's life and work.

In practice, some missions will accept young people in their very early twenties. But it is generally held that 25 or 26 is a much better age to enter the work. It gives time for more thorough preparation and the needed maturity.

Again, many missions set 30 as the maximum age for a candidate under normal conditions. Others extend the limit to 35, especially where more preparation is required. This maximum age limit is set aside in some exceptional cases. It may be done for doctors, for instance. The reason is that their period of training is quite prolonged. Also the effectiveness of their ministry is not quite so closely tied up with their ability to use the native tongue as that of the evangelistic missionary. It may also be done for others with specialized training. That is, it will be done if their special abilities are needed badly enough to offset the disadvantage of their age.

Now a word about health. The average missionary works in fields and under conditions that make serious demands on his health and strength. The mortality rate among missionaries has been greatly reduced in recent years, and the conditions of work in most fields have been improved, but the job still calls for a sound and vigorous constitution.

Then too, in spite of the noble work being done in many fields by the medical missionaries, and in spite of the growth of a better native medical practice, there are still many places where the missionary can't count on competent help in illness. Sometimes the non-medical missionary not only has to take care of his own family, but from his limited knowledge of medicine he has to try to help the sick among the natives.

Of course there are wide differences between fields, and each mission sets its standards according to the need in its own field. But in principle, the candidate needs to be sound and robust when he leaves for his field of service. He will have to be able to adjust himself readily to a new climate and environment, to carry on an active life, and to take up the heavy responsibilities of his mission without undue strain. He must have the health to combat any unforeseen illness that attacks him, with reasonable hopes of success.

To assure this, the missions usually prescribe a rigid physical examination for each candidate. The mission itself prefers to choose the doctor who makes the examination rather than depend on the candidate's family physician. The reason is obvious. Sometimes for greater security they require more than one examination.

It is not at all uncommon for the examining doctor to find some dormant ailment of which the candidate was not aware. And some of these things can easily flare up into activity under the strains of missionary life. Some ailments can be corrected with little difficulty, though the treatment may delay the candidate's acceptance or departure for the field. Others are more serious.

For this reason, if you are thinking of foreign missionary service, it may be well to have a complete physical check-up at the earliest opportunity. Do it even before applying to the mission or finishing your course of training. That is, of course, unless you are already on the verge of applying. It may be that only in a few cases will the examination reveal an unsuspected illness that would close the door to foreign service. But there is no keener disappointment than that of the young person who has dedicated his life for foreign missions, has spent a number of years in preparation, has built up his plans and hopes about it, and then discovers through the final medical examination that he can't go.

In speaking of health the average layman is likely to overlook matters of nervous and mental stability. So let me add a word just here. By experience the missions have learned to take these things into consideration. Excessive nervousness at home becomes greatly aggravated under the strains of missionary life. It may even become dangerous. And of course mental health and balance are, if anything, more necessary for an effective ministry than bodily soundness. The mental and spiritual strains of missionary life are greater than the physical strains. They can scarcely be comprehended by one who has not actually served on the field and experienced them.

A further practical note. One of the most important factors in preserving missionary health is personal cleanliness and neatness. This is largely a matter of habits, habits that can be built up before going to the field and adjusted to meet the conditions there. Slovenliness is both irritating to those you have to live with, and it opens the door to needless disease.

Do keep this in mind. A condition that would keep you from the field today, you may often so correct that within a year or two it would no longer stand in the way. The very experience of overcoming your handicap is the best possible training for service on the field.

Of course there are some physical handicaps that you can't completely overcome. The loss of a leg or an arm, or the crippling effects of poliomyelitis are permanent handicaps. They sometimes close the door to missionary service. But not always. There are some places and kinds of work where the possession of two arms or two legs is not essential. Then, if you have the special ability or training that is needed, you may find the mission ready to overlook your handicap. Teaching in an established station, or literary work, are just two of several types of service that a handicapped person can perform. But of course you have to be superior in your abilities so as to compensate for the handicap.

The matter of educational requirements calls for special attention. It is perhaps more misunderstood than any other requirement.

Missionary work is first of all a spiritual service. As such there can never be any satisfactory substitute for a real personal knowledge and experience of Christ. No amount of education can cover up a lack here. If we had to choose between a candidate with little formal education but a vital relationship to Jesus Christ, and another with a very high scholastic record but a very superficial experience of the power of the Gospel, the choice would be easy. The first would make by far the better missionary.

But such a theoretical case probably never occurs. What does often occur is that the mission must choose between candidates whose religious experience is more or less similar, but whose educational qualifications may differ widely. Given the same amount of spiritual life and leadership, the one with the better educational background is sure to prove more useful on the field.

Missionary work makes great demands on the intellectual ability and preparation of the missionary. Some types of work demand more than others, but they all demand an ability that is definitely above average. We find the reason in the work the missionary has to do. His ministry is largely mental and spiritual.

Sometimes we get absorbed in the physical side of missionary life. We like to hear of the missionary's adventures, his physical hardships, the problems of living in another land. But these are only incidental. They are interesting but not fundamental. Missionaries at times get irritated because people are always asking what they have to eat. "As if that were all that mattered!" exclaimed one missionary in disgust. "Why don't they ask about the work?"

Of course sometimes the missionary's work does include building, repairing, and traveling, and a good many other such activities. But those are not the real purpose of his being there. His main job is dealing with the souls of men. It may not take most of his time, but it is the heart of his work.

He tries to sway men's thinking. He seeks to change the course and objectives of their lives. The arms of his warfare are spiritual. Words are his most valuable weapons—preëminently the Word of God. He plants thoughts and nourishes them until they bear fruit. The fruits of his labors are changed hearts and minds. He stimulates the fellowship of the saints and guides their worship. With wise counsel he multiplies his usefulness and sees recreated in others that spiritual life and development that Christ has already brought to him. He deals in thoughts, in souls, in life.

To do this he must be prepared. And while the years of school work don't always show the amount of training a man has, we don't have any other very usable gauge. So missions will continue to use this one. They will keep on stating this requirement in terms of years of schooling, courses taken and degrees obtained.

Remember this. The missionary usually has to do his work in a language other than his own. He has to learn that language, not superficially so as to bargain in the market place or to give orders to a construction gang, but thoroughly. Remember that he has to teach the people *in their own tongue* the sublime truths of Christianity, the most profound truths the human mind is capable of grasping. Unless the people understand his message, all his work is in vain. Among primitive people his task is even more difficult than among those who are more advanced. It is always true that the greatest simplicity of expression calls for the greatest depth and breadth of knowledge.

Remember too, that a missionary, no matter how humbly he may want to serve, soon finds that he has to take a place of leadership. His work demands it. And while leaders may occasionally come from among the self-educated, they never come from the ranks of the uneducated.

Besides, it is a mistake always to think of missionary work in terms of ignorant, uncultured, primitive peoples. We have a marvelous message to give, but we mustn't get it confused with our blind pride in being superior to every other people. Really we aren't. We have much to learn from others. Even from the so-called "primitives."

But the fact is that in many of the "backward" areas the missionary has to deal with some very well-educated people. We need to remember that many mission fields, just like our own country, are not static. They are changing, too. They are improving their educational systems. Many of their young people have even studied in our own colleges and universities.

It is no wonder that some missionaries, after a time on the field, begin to feel a lack in their educational background. Some are enrolled in our schools right now. They have even asked for extended furloughs so they can complete the education they lacked before going out. Or they take additional work to improve their ministry.

In reality, the educational *needs* for a foreign missionary are greater than those for the home worker. He does the same work and more. He has to do it in another language. The circumstances are much less favorable. And he has to get along with only a fraction of the equipment available at home. Or, what is quite common, he will improvise, invent or manufacture his own.

The principle involved in the educational requirement is this: Education should be preparation for living. Therefore the missionary must have an education that will help him to live among the people in a way that will gain their respect. But education is also preparation for service. So the missionary must have enough education, and of the right kind, to prepare him for his part of the missionary job.

This is very broad, I know. The reason is that missionary work itself is so broad. Different kinds of work call for different kinds of training. And some ministries require longer preparation than others. In general, a broad cultural education, plus Bible training, gives the best foundation.

In practice, most of the denominational missions require their candidates to graduate from a four-year college course. In addition, they require seminary or Bible institute of those who are not going to engage in some specialized work, such as medicine, general education, agriculture, etc. Even for this specialized work they may require at least a year of Bible training, since all these efforts must contribute to the chief missionary aim.

The faith missions, and some small denominations, set a minimum requirement of graduation from high school, plus Bible institute training. This is a minimum, and they may recommend more. In fact, the trend among the better established faith missions is toward a raising of these requirements.

For specialized work of course there are special requirements. Some are set by the mission and some by the country to which the missionary goes. The Mission, for example, will insist that its doctors be fully qualified to practice in their homeland. They want their educational missionaries to have the proper training to make them good teachers. The governments, in addition, may make other demands. For instance, in Nigeria any missionary who dispenses medicines must have taken at least six months of certain prescribed courses of study in this field and be certified by the government. In the Belgian Congo, those who conduct schools recognized by the government must take certain courses in Belgium. Since these requirements differ a great deal from place to place and from time to time, you need to have the advice of the mission's candidate secretary during the period of training.

We have said that missionary work demands an ability that is definitely above average. This doesn't mean that every missionary is expected to be an intellectual genius. Each one of course will show more talent in one direction than another, but it is better to have a well-rounded development than extreme brilliance in a limited field. A high average scholarship, in spite of a few low grades, is good. And one of the most valuable traits is an aptitude for teaching others.

CHAPTER XIII

MISSIONARY QUALIFICATIONS
(*Concluded*)

BESIDES ITS PHYSICAL and educational requirements, the mission is always interested in the personality of the one who seeks appointment.

Our present-day use of the term "personality" is very hard to define. It seems to be the total effect of our manner of acting upon others. So we say a man has no personality if he fails to make any deep impression, either good or bad, on others. He has a good personality if his good qualities, as we see them, impress us more strongly than his bad ones. And a bad personality is just the reverse.

These things don't have to bear any relation to reality. The man with the good personality may be a scoundrel of deepest dye, and the one with no personality may have the strongest character of the lot. We are dealing only with the outward appearance and the impression it makes on others. The Scripture recognizes this difference between the reality of an action and the impression it makes on others. It says, "Let not your good be evil spoken of." It urges us both to do good and to see that the impression is good.

A bookkeeper doesn't have to worry about the impression he makes on anybody but the boss. The main thing is to have his records neat and accurate. That's not true of the salesperson, however. The volume of his sales and the commission he gets may depend on such impressions. A research scientist may be a very disagreeable person to meet, at the same time that he is highly regarded for his contributions to science. But a minister of the Gospel can't even get a hearing for his message if he continually rubs people the wrong way.

The missionary, of all people, needs to make the right kind of impressions. He not only has to get a hearing for his message, but that message is so tied in with his own life that the impression of his life and the impression of the Gospel are likely to be the same thing. Then, too, his whole ministry revolves around his relationship with other people. He can't do his work in a corner.

Even such a scholarly task as the translation of the Bible requires contact with the people. The translator has to immerse himself in the life of the people until he can express the living message of the Bible in the living tongue that they use every day. He has to draw out from them the words that he needs, with infinite patience and understanding. But he can't do it until he wins first their confidence.

Then add to these things the fact that the missionary must both work *and live* with other missionaries under conditions that are not the best. And this relationship is not one that he can terminate on two weeks' notice.

No wonder the mission is very much interested in the personality of its candidates.

If you ask what elements in the personality are the most important, no one can say. Perhaps no two missionary leaders would agree on a list of them. Even when there is fairly general agreement on one trait, we have to admit that there have been some outstanding exceptions. That is, there have been some who lacked that trait, or were weak in it, and still made good missionaries.

The reason is that personality is not a collection of independent traits. It is a composite in which the many traits are fused together into a whole being. We like one man and we dislike another without stopping to analyze their personalities and determine just what elements we like or dislike in them. When we weigh them in the balance of our likes and dislikes, we never estimate just how much generosity it takes to counterbalance an ounce of jealousy. We just react to the total impression they make on us.

It is to get that total impression that some missions don't depend wholly on the questionnaires they send to the candidate and his references. The questionnaire only deals with definite and specific items. They don't even depend on a few personal interviews, which are more general and allow them to get some personal impressions. But they try to arrange for a longer personal contact with him in the affairs of daily life. They invite him to spend a time in the mission home—maybe a week or so, maybe a longer period. There he lives, works and studies with other candidates. They see how he gets along with others. They get a general view of his personality.

There are some things about the personality of the candidate that the mission is particularly interested in. Sometimes they ask questions of the references; sometimes they get the answers in other ways. I have stated the questions so that the preferred answer is obvious. Then the candidate can look them over, check his own weaknesses and perhaps make some improvements.

(1) Does the candidate have real strength of character? Or does he usually run along with the crowd and let others make his decisions for him?

(2) Is he self-centered, or does he take a real interest in the affairs of others?

(3) Is he easily discouraged by difficulties? Does he usually finish what he begins?

(4) Does he work well when not under supervision? Can he be depended on to fulfill all his obligations?

(5) Is he usually tactful and reasonable, even under moderate stress? Or does he easily lose his head?

(6) Does he have a good supply of common sense?

(7) Does he show the initiative and willingness to take responsibility that a leader needs?

(8) Is it difficult for him to co-operate with others, or to obey those in authority?

(9) Does he readily adapt himself to new situations?

(10) Has he learned to endure hardness *without complaint?*

(11) What about his emotional stability? Is he given to fits of despondency? Does he have a good sense of humor?

(12) Can he stand criticism, and even ridicule?

(13) Is he willing to serve in any capacity if necessary, no matter how humble?

(14) Does he have a teachable spirit?

Now a word about Christian life and work as a qualification.

The spiritual qualifications we began with are essential for missionary service. But, as we said, the mission board would find it hard to evaluate them. For practical purposes they inquire into certain definite matters about the candidate's life and experience.

Of course they want to know first of all if he has given evidence of real Christian life and character. They ask this of his references and any others who may know him.

Then they want to know from the candidate if he has any definite convictions about the missionary call, motives and purposes. Why does he want to be a missionary?

In the matter of beliefs there is quite a difference of procedure. Some missions require the candidate simply to sign the doctrinal statement of the mission. Some want an independent statement from the candidate himself in his own words. Some quiz him on certain special items. The whole purpose is to make sure that he is in harmony with the fundamental principles of the mission.

Experience in Christian work is very important. The missionary shouldn't go out as a novice. If he hasn't learned to

serve Christ and to win souls in his homeland, he isn't ready
for overseas service. Sometimes a mission will even recommend that he have a short period in the pastorate or in the
home mission field before he is approved to go abroad.

One last question is frequently put to the candidate in
somewhat this form: "What are your devotional habits?
(Note that we say *habits,* not occasional practices.)" Our devotional practices are very deliberate in their beginning, and
the atmosphere in which most young people live is not very
conducive to keeping them up with regularity. It is only
through constant repetition over a long period of time that
they become habitual. Then they show the mold into which
the spiritual life has been cast.

Engagement and marriage must next be considered.

It may seem strange that the matter of engagement and marriage should come under the heading of qualifications for
missionary service. But it has a definite bearing on the subject. In considering the qualifications of a candidate, the mission always wants to know whether he is married, engaged or
single. It makes a difference. They don't want single missionaries for some kinds of work. For others they do. They may
even consider that some candidates would be acceptable if
married; otherwise not. And of course if there are children it
may influence the decision.

The great majority of missionaries are married, either before leaving for the field or at some time afterward. The mission seldom makes it a requirement today, but it figures on it
as the usual thing. In some cases it may even prefer married
couples. This is especially true in places where custom demands that all women must have husbands and any unat-
tached woman is not respectable. But marriage does present
some problems that each candidate needs to understand.

There are some very real values in having a missionary
family on most fields. So the mission, as such, is not usually
opposed to marriage or families. Neither does it presume to

judge whether the young man's intended is the right one for him. That is a purely personal matter. But these things do have an effect on the work. And that is what concerns the mission. Let's see if we can make the problems clear.

One of the problems became especially acute shortly after World War II. That war interrupted or postponed the training of many young men for missionary service. On their return from military service, after several years of absence, it was only natural that many of them should decide to get married before continuing their training. The government itself favored such an arrangement by increasing its educational allowance to those who had wives and families.

In time these young couples applied for appointment to the mission field. One day the director of a large mission said to me, "What are we going to do with these young couples who apply to us with three or four children? We don't want to turn a man down simply because he has a family. But you can see the problems it raises."

Of course I could. It means a much larger expenditure for outfit and passage. It means more support on the field during the long months of learning the language, getting introduced to the many phases of the work and becoming adjusted. It means not only increased problems of housing during language school days, but also the problem of caring for the children so that the parents may have time for classes and study. It means all the burdens and distractions of caring for a sizable family at the time when the young couple should be giving their attention to getting a grasp of the work.

But in spite of such problems, the missions do send out a number of families, especially where they are very well qualified. The most conservative will accept those with only one child. Others have no set rule and consider each case on its individual merits.

Aside from the problems presented by the children, the candidate ought to understand that the mission usually expects both the man and his wife to be missionaries. Sometimes a mission will appoint a missionary and his wife; but usually they prefer to appoint two missionaries. The wife is expected to measure up to the usual standards of acceptance. Her ministry will not be just the same as if she were single, and it shouldn't make her neglect her family responsibilities, but it is a real ministry. And it requires real ability and good preparation.

What does a mission do when, for health or some other reason, one of the two is not acceptable? What can it do but reject them both? It is a hard decision to make, but it is necessary. It has been made many a time.

For the young couple this may seem like a tragic disappointment. But it doesn't need to be. If you have let the Lord lead you in the choice of your helpmate just as sincerely as in the other affairs of life; if you are sure that He has brought you two together and means for you to be together; then the rejection can only mean that He has another place of service for you. You should consider such a rejection in the same light as if it had been the rejection of both individuals. For in God's sight you two are in truth "one flesh."

It is customary for missions to require that couples be married for at least a year before actually sailing for the field. The major purpose is quite simple, yet important. Marriage involves many adjustments in the lives of the young couple, adjustments they don't often think about ahead of time. Little things like the time for meals, or what to do of an evening, or whether to buy a new rug for the living-room, can no longer be decided by each one individually. And there are a hundred and one other adjustments in the blending of two hitherto independent lives.

Also when we go to foreign lands as missionaries of Christ there are many adjustments to make. There is a different climate, different conditions of living, a very different people whose ways of thinking seem strange to us. There is a new etiquette to learn and abide by, a new lack of privacy even in our own home, and a radically new diet to get used to.

To make two sets of adjustments of such a radical nature at one and the same time is too much to require of anyone. In addition, the honeymoon is not the best time for learning a new and difficult language. So at least a year is allowed for adjustment to married life before the adjustment to missionary life is begun.

A similar situation faces those engaged young people who go to the field single, expecting to be married after they arrive. But here it is the adjustment to missionary life that they need to make before they enter into marriage. The mission usually requires them to wait one or two years after they reach the field. That is, they wait until the adjustment to the field has been made and the language has been learned.

There is a further complication for the engaged couples. The mission has found that it is wise to put them in separate stations until marriage. That means they don't have the frequent opportunities to see one another that they enjoyed in the homeland. It also means that one of the stations is going to lose a worker just at the time when he is becoming really useful. Or maybe after marriage they will both be sent to an entirely different station. But this problem is unavoidable.

If you ask whether it is better to get married before going to the field, or wait until after arriving, you will get all sorts of answers. No one will fit all cases. The idea of getting married first is usually the more attractive. But the mission will point out several dangers. There is a danger that you may get sidetracked into some other line of service while you are waiting. Or the arrival of children may postpone your leaving for the field; or it may preclude it altogether. Each candidate has to make his own decision in the light of all the facts, and looking to the Lord for guidance.

CHAPTER XIV

MISSIONARY PREPARATION

H OW DOES A YOUNG PERSON go about getting prepared for missionary service? The answer to this question is not easy. You see, it depends to some extent on the point in his life at which he makes his decision to volunteer. Maybe he is already near the age limit. Then there isn't much time for special training, though he may already have some training that is useful. But if he makes his decision in his teens, he will have plenty of time to carry out a thorough, well-planned course of preparation.

Still, there are other things to consider. He wants to be a missionary. But what kind of missionary? Maybe he has only a vague idea of what a missionary is and does. Is he to be an evangelistic missionary? An educational missionary? A medical missionary? A technical missionary? Each of these requires special aptitudes and preparation.

The personal characteristics and abilities of the young person enter into the problem, too. Just because you think you would like to be a missionary doctor doesn't mean that you can be one. And don't think that you are fitted for "pioneer work" simply because the stories of such work always give you a thrill.

There are a good many missionary training schools; some good, some not so good. They range all the way from a few months in a so-called "boot camp" to the specialized work in some graduate schools of missions. But none of them does the whole job. They build on a basis of previous training. Some don't have any requirements of previous education. But they still take it for granted that you have had our ordinary public school training. Others have most of their students with degrees from colleges and seminaries. What they are able to do depends both on their own program and on what their students have learned before.

But much of the training for a missionary doesn't come from schools or books. It is gained in other ways. And success in missionary work depends fully as much on this extracurricular preparation as it does on the school work. For a missionary is a witness to Christ and to the Christian life. So he must know that life by living it.

There are several things in missionary preparation that we might call indispensables. That is, they are not only important, but so valuable that to miss them would cause our ministry to suffer. They are things so fundamental that without them there can't be a real missionary ministry at all. They are things we can't do without. Let's take a little time to talk about them. Then I think you will see what we mean.

It may seem strange to say that there is any particular kind of preparation that *all* missionaries ought to have for *all* fields. Even more strange to say that there is any type of preparation that is really indispensable for them all. After all, there is a great deal of specialization in missions today. There has to be. And surely the technical specialist doesn't need the same kind of preparation as the evangelistic missionary.

In a sense he doesn't. His training as a technician is quite different from that of the evangelist. But remember that he is a *missionary*. And if the word *missionary* is to have any meaning at all, it must mean that those who bear that name have some things in common. It is those things which make them missionaries. It is like those who call themselves Christians. By occupation they may be almost anything. But in that name they are united in a common faith, a common standard of right and wrong, etc.

The true indispensables in missionary preparation are all spiritual. Classroom work plays a part, but it is not effective by itself. It is too easy to learn lessons for an examination without having them affect the course of our lives. We can take the finest course of preparation offered in any school and still be unprepared for missionary service. Some have done it. We need something more, something in addition to the school work.

In general there are four indispensables in the preparation of the missionary. First, and fundamental to all the rest, there is the training of our inner life—what we might call spiritual training. Then there is the training to show forth that life in our relation to others, a matter of vital importance in all missionary service. A third item is, of course, our training in the message we are called to deliver. A missionary is God's messenger, so he must have His message well in hand. And last is the matter of experience, which comes from practice in presenting the message to others. Experience also brings maturity, that seasoning which we can only get by actually coming to grips with life and living men.

In the vitally important line of spiritual training the least systematic work has been done. The mission boards look for certain spiritual qualifications in those who apply, but the schools don't offer courses in the subject. It may be that we are counting on the churches' doing the job. If so, we're making a big mistake. The training given by most churches is quite haphazard. And when several young people offer themselves for missions from the same church, the amount of spiritual training they have had is never the same.

One candidate, for instance, was born in a devout Christian home. At an early age he accepted the Saviour. Shortly afterward he offered his life for service on the foreign mission field. This allows for years of development before he actually sails. The Bible becomes a familiar book; family devotions and private prayers make their mark on his life; Sunday school lessons, sermons, conferences, Bible camps, young people's societies, all help to foster and strengthen the growth of his spiritual life.

Another, however, did not know of Christ's salvation until some time during his college days. He comes from a non-Christian background and has already delved deeply into the sinful ways of the world. But then he allows Christ to enter his life and it is transformed. In the enthusiasm of his new-found faith he too volunteers for missionary service. He hasn't the background of the first candidate, but he is not a whit behind him in sincerity of purpose. He may even excel him in warm-hearted zeal. He joins the church and takes an active part in its affairs. He associates with other Christian young people. He takes counsel with his pastor and drinks in avidly the messages that he hears.

Now it is possible that the second young man may outstrip the first in his spiritual development after a time. Then again, maybe he won't. It is something that is hard to prophesy. In any case he is not likely to find that any course has been planned for his spiritual development. Certainly not in college. Even in the seminary they aim chiefly to give him an intellectual mastery of certain truths and to help him gain certain skills. His spiritual profiting will depend mostly on his own initiative and his associations outside of the classroom.

Of all preparatory schools, the Bible institutes seem to have made the most definite provision for training of the spirit as well as the mind. Of course it is not enough. They themselves would be the first to admit it. But it is a part of their plan, and an important one. Student life is more closely regulated than in other schools. There is an emphasis, often repeated, on the devotional life and practical Christianity. Every student is assigned to do some practical Christian service, which makes him exercise the spiritual life he already has and helps him grow. But even so, it is not enough.

What kind of spiritual training does the missionary need? Let me mention briefly a few items with which not many will disagree. Devotional habits are very important—habits of communing with God in prayer and drawing help and instruction and inspiration from His Word. These are almost the breath of life to the missionary. Now it takes constant and regular repetition to turn an occasional practice into a habit. This is part of our missionary preparation.

With these habits should go the constant application of Christian principles to everyday living. A course in Christian ethics at school is not of much value so long as it is kept in the abstract. The principles don't begin to have real meaning and value until they are applied to definite situations. For instance, it is easy to repeat that all lying is wrong. But it is not so easy to tell the truth when a lie would apparently save you from an embarrassing situation. How do you know the principle is true if you don't apply it? A missionary must be sure!

Also, what good is it to know the theological definition of faith, or to be able to expound Paul's teaching on faith in Galatians, if you don't know how to exercise faith in the affairs of life? There are many times, even in student life, when faith is called for. And do take notice that, to the heathen, religion is fully as much experience as it is theory, if not more so. He won't be interested in any new theory or doctrine that isn't borne out by experience.

Training for your own spirit also comes through learning to deal with others about their soul's needs. Here our first indispensable merges with the others, especially with the second one, the one that deals with our relationship with other people. Personal evangelism is the very cornerstone of missionary work everywhere, and the same preparation of heart that you need for it here at home is what you need in foreign lands. Personal counseling, too, is one of the missionary's most common jobs, and one of the most demanding. Its principles are pretty much the same wherever you go. And one of those principles is that the counselor must show a real interest in the one who seeks his help. In fact, the missionary needs to be, of all people, one who is unselfishly interested in others, one who is willing to make their burdens his own.

In a missionary's life, too, relationship to others involves the matter of leadership. For whether he wants it or not, people do look to him for leadership. Now some seem to think that leadership is a purely natural gift; that some people are born leaders while others will always be followers. It's perfectly true that some do have an exceptional talent for leadership. But it is not true that all of our leaders come from those talented few. Instead, it is perfectly possible for those who don't have such a gift to develop real ability as leaders. Often all that they need is the opportunity and the encouragement to step out and lead.

We said that missionaries are expected to be leaders. Whether they get proper training beforehand or not, the very circumstances of their life make them take on the responsibilities of leadership. If they have had good training and experience, they can do a creditable job. If not, they will probably become petty dictators. And this will bring harm to the work.

What does leadership training involve? We can give only a limited amount in class instruction; we can explain some of the basic principles and how to apply them. The student can learn more by observing those who lead, by following their example. But more important than either of these is experience in leading. The one who wants to be a leader needs to take every chance to exercise leadership.

Several things are fundamental. The leader needs to have a definite objective; he must know where he is going. He has to be ready to make decisions, and then accept the responsibility for them after they are made. The one who finds it hard to make up his mind, who always hesitates to commit himself for fear he might make a mistake, had better practice making decisions on every possible occasion. He will make mistakes, of course. But his mistakes will be just so many valuable lessons that will help him to make better decisions next time. And the one who doesn't want to take responsibility just isn't material for a missionary.

The one who is to be a Christian leader also needs to learn the lesson that Peter taught, that we are to take the oversight of God's flock, not "as being lords over God's heritage, but being ensamples to the flock." We show real leadership when we can get others to do what we have in mind, while all the time they are convinced that they are doing what they want.

Our third indispensable has to do with the mastery of the message we bear to others. All too often I have been asked by those who had some special technical training or skill, "Is there a place where I can be used in the mission field?" They usually presume that in missionary work we need laboratory technicians, printers, builders, teachers, nurses, etc. That is all wrong. We need *missionaries*—young men and young women with a message! They may be educational missionaries, industrial missionaries, medical missionaries; but first and foremost they must be missionaries. As a doctor in the Congo once wrote, "If I thought my job out here was just to heal men's bodies, I would stay at home!"

All of the various types of work in which missionaries engage are proper and useful only as they contribute to the one great aim of missions. They must be related to the task of bringing Christ to the people, of winning them to Him and building them up in Him.

Every missionary must be a man with a message, and he must know that message well. The mission field is no place for the man who has serious doubts about his faith. Neither is it the place for one who is not quite sure just what his message is. He doesn't have to be a finished theologian. He doesn't need to be a profound student of the prophetic Word. But he does need to know the essential elements of his faith and be fully persuaded of their truth. He does have to show to the people that he has a working knowledge of the Scriptures. And he must be able to show them how that message touches their lives.

Remember that the people to whom the missionary goes are not ignorant. They may be illiterate, but that is quite another thing. There are often among illiterate people some of the keenest minds to be found anywhere. And they are remarkably acute in their evaluation of the missionary. They may overlook his halting speech, his apparent lack of logic in some of the things he says, and even his ignorance of some things that don't have too much to do with his work. But two faults are inexcusable: a failure to know his message, and an insincerity in professing what he doesn't fully believe or practice.

Bible training, then, is indispensable to all missionaries, no matter what their type of service.

Our final indispensable is experience in presenting the message. We have already said something about maturity in the spiritual life, which comes through experience. We have also spoken of experience in such a matter as the leadership of others. The Bible, too, becomes a living message to others largely to the extent that we who preach it have experienced its power in our own lives. It is remarkable how these indispensable elements in missionary preparation are intertwined with one another. It is only in our thinking that we attempt to separate them. In life they merge into one another.

This matter of experience in presenting the message is very important. Mr. Moody knew its value and stressed it in founding the Moody Bible Institute. He made practical Christian work an integral part of the course of training. It still has that place of importance at Moody as well as in other Bible institutes.

Yet in spite of such experience during their school days, I have had students come to me as they neared graduation and say, "I don't believe I'm ready to go out as a missionary. If I am to be a leader on the mission field I feel that I need more experience in dealing with souls, more experience in meeting the spiritual problems of real life." And some of these young people have gone into home mission work for a short time to get that experience before going abroad.

Such young people have shown a real perception of what it means to be a missionary. On the mission field you are not reciting lessons. People don't quiz you on the subjects you had in school and allow you to show why you got top honors in theology or church history or some other such subject. In fact, what may disturb the missionary most is their complete indifference to what he has to say, even when they are polite enough to listen while he talks.

You are a missionary. So what? That doesn't mean anything to them except that you are an object of curiosity. Can you engage them in conversation and so direct that conversation that it will turn to matters of the spirit? It's not difficult in many fields. Other peoples are often more interested in religious matters than are the folks at home. But once you have begun the discussion, can you keep it in the main channel where you can present the Lord Jesus Christ in all His desirability? Can you disregard the minor matters and get to the heart of the question so as to reach the heart of the man? It takes practice.

Again, missionary leaders are insisting, "We need missionaries who know how to express themselves!" Well, that is just where experience comes in. You don't learn to express yourself by reading a book or answering a set of true-false questions. You need practice. If, as they say, you "learn to write by writing," you also learn to express yourself by repeated efforts to tell others what is in your mind.

The aim of missions is not simply to proclaim the Gospel. It is to proclaim it in such a way that men will listen to it, understand it, and be moved to obey it. Differences of language don't mean very much in this matter. If you can express yourself in English you will learn to express yourself in another tongue. If your thoughts are hazy and disordered, and your expression is anything but clear in English, there is no magic in learning another language that will straighten you out. You need this preparation before going to the field.

One last thing. We have mentioned the missionary's need to give counsel on the field, counsel of all sorts. More than anything else, this calls for experience. You need to know people through much association with them. The missionary is no hermit. You need to know something of the forces that move men, the problems that most of them face. It takes experience as well as tact to draw them out and to avoid the pitfalls that go with snap judgments. "Advice is cheap," we say, for there is so much cheap advice on the market. It is given without any background of experience to make it valuable. Yet when a troubled new believer comes to a young missionary with a vital problem, he doesn't want cheap advice. He has come to God's messenger and he looks for God's message. How humble it should make the missionary feel, and how dependent on God!

These things, then, are indispensable in the preparation of the missionary candidate. Other training is useful, but this is fundamental. Some of it can be given in the school curriculum, and perhaps we can do more along that line. Some can be given in the church, if the church is alert to its opportunities.

But much of it, in fact the very heart of the whole matter, depends on the individual. The candidate must not expect others to prepare him for the mission field. They will do what they can, but it is limited. On the candidate himself rests the responsibility of such a close walk with God, and such a full determination to serve Him well, that the Holy Spirit, the master teacher, can accomplish that indispensable work of preparation which is His own special ministry.

CHAPTER XV

MISSIONARY PREPARATION
(*Continued*)

THERE IS NO ONE COURSE of preparation for all missionary service. There can't be. The things that missionaries do are too varied. Their fields and the requirements of their work are too different.

Two missionaries to Central America took identical courses of missionary preparation. The course included some elementary medical and dental instruction. It might seem that if either one of them needed that training, the other would need it, too. But it didn't turn out that way.

Here is what they told me. One had worked in and around the capital of his country. At the end of his second term of service he said, "I've never had to use a day of that medical instruction I took." The other had his field among the lowland Indians of the Caribbean coast. After an even shorter period of service he said, "With just that little bit of dental instruction, I have already pulled a thousand teeth."

This seems quite confusing. How are you going to know what training to get? How can you tell which course of preparation to follow? Is there an answer that will cover most cases?

There is indeed. It is a three-fold answer. First, there is some training that is indispensable. We have already talked about this. Then, there is some training that is so generally needed that nearly everybody ought to get it. We'll talk about this in a moment. And finally, there is some training that depends on the needs of a particular field or mission; or it depends on your own talents and interests. This last is the most difficult to talk about. Every case is different. Not only do they face different circumstances, but not many young people are really aware of their own abilities and limitations.

Now let's give attention to the more generally needed types of training.

First is the matter of language. We've already said that to be able to express yourself in English is indispensable. To be able to learn to do it in another language is almost as important. There are not very many fields where you can use English effectively in missionary work. Not even in places like Nigeria where English is taught in the schools. Educated people there do learn to read, write and speak English; but a message in English doesn't mean as much to them as a message in their native tongue. As an educated Filipino said to me one day, "English speaks to our heads; but our own language speaks to our hearts!"

"That's all right," someone will say; "you ought to do a good job studying the language on the field. But what can you do about it here in the homeland? How can you fit it into a course of preparation? Our schools don't teach many languages."

That's perfectly true. There aren't many cases where you can study here the language you will use in the field. But that's no excuse for omitting language study completely from your course of training. In fact, some mission boards will insist that you have some language study before they consider your application. They want to know if you're likely to be able to learn another language. Besides, the study of any other language than our own has real value. It helps us to see that *differences of language are not just differences of words.* They are different ways of thinking and of expressing thought. If you have once learned one foreign language you will find it much easier to undertake others.

It isn't hard to get a foreign language in your course of preparation. Nearly all our high schools provide training in one or more foreign languages. As likely as not, you will have to take one in order to enter college. And you may have to take two years in some language to graduate. Some Bible institutes also offer foreign languages.

For missionaries it is usually best to choose the modern languages. That is because they are actually spoken today. They are usually taught in a somewhat different way from the dead languages, with more emphasis on pronunciation and conversation. But in some cases the dead languages may be more useful. If you are going to do translation work, that is, translation of the Bible, then study Greek and Hebrew. It will help you do a better job.

Sometimes you can study at home a language that you will use on your field. Then do it. You can get Spanish in nearly all of our high schools and colleges. And Spanish is what you will use in most of Latin America. French is also taught in most of our colleges and in many high schools. You will need French in large parts of Africa. Portuguese is not so commonly taught, but it is given in a number of schools. It is useful for Brazil and for the large Portuguese possessions in Africa. In fact, no matter where you learn it, you are going to have to know Portuguese before you will be admitted to Angola or Mozambique. The language requirement for French Africa is not quite so strict, but some day it may be. The missions themselves make a practice of sending their missionaries first to France or Belgium for language study before they go on to French Africa or the Belgian Congo. If you need another language, such as Japanese, Chinese or Arabic, you will have a harder time getting it. There are not many schools that teach these languages.

There was a time when many missionaries advised against

the study of a native language in the homeland. Some of them still do. They usually mention two reasons. One is that you don't learn the language correctly, especially when it comes to pronunciation. You need to live among the people to get it right. The other is that you start talking on the field before you know the people and know what is wise to say.

There is a good deal of truth in both these reasons. The trouble is that their importance has been exaggerated. That is, in spite of our better methods of language teaching, it is still true that many foreign language teachers don't really speak well the language they are teaching. They learned it in school themselves and never had to use it in everyday life. But they make most of their mistakes in pronunciation and idiom. They are usually able to give a good foundation in grammar.

Now when you take a language in school, you don't usually get enough of it to develop any very fixed habits of pronunciation. That is, any bad habits are not so fixed that you can't readily correct them later. On the other hand, see what our actual experience has been. Some missionaries have studied the language before going to the field. And in no case has it been a hindrance to them. Instead, they have usually been able to take part in the work sooner than others.

Also it is true that a new missionary who knows how to speak the language might possibly say some unwise things. It's possible, but it doesn't often happen. The reason is that he is usually afraid to say very much. Nearly every new missionary has to be encouraged to talk. He is even afraid to go out on the street for fear someone will talk to *him,* and he may not understand.

Missionaries often do make slips of the tongue. But it is not just the new missionaries. Neither is it noticeable that those who learned some of the language at home make any more than the others.

We have said that some people exaggerate the disadvan-

tages of studying the language in the homeland. We don't
want to go to the other extreme and exaggerate the advantages. There are some advantages. They are very real advantages. They warrant your taking classes in the language while
you are preparing for the field. If the course is a concentrated
one, it might even warrant delaying your departure so as to
take it. But don't spend a year or more after you are ready for
the field just taking one of our ordinary language courses. You
can do better on the field.

Here are some of the advantages of studying at home. First,
it will give you a grasp of the grammatical foundations of the
language. Then it won't be entirely strange and confusing to
you when you first get to the field. Those first days are confusing enough, with all the new things you have to learn and
get used to.

Then, such study will take you through the first period of
discouragement. There always comes a time when you think
you will never get the language, a time when you wonder
how anyone could ever learn to talk such stuff. Better to un-
dergo that first discouragement here than out there.

A third advantage is that the study may shorten your stay
in the language school. This means that you will be able to
take part in the work sooner. It will save time and money for
you and your supporters.

And we haven't said anything about the attitude of the
people to whom you go. You will find that they deeply appreciate those who can speak to them in their own tongue
from the beginning, even though imperfectly.

Perhaps we ought to note what the British government does
with its young men for the colonial service. It sends them to
the School of Oriental and African languages in London to
get training in the language they need. In fact, the school itself owes much to the co-operation of the government. Yet, if
anything, the missionary has greater need than the civil servant for such training.

But there are many languages that can't be studied in the homeland, especially in the United States. Some of them are not taught in our schools. Some have not yet been reduced to written form. For missionaries who go to places where these languages are used, other courses are available.

A course in general phonetics, particularly if it has a missionary slant, is valuable for all missionaries. Phonetics deals with the sounds of human speech. In such a course you learn about the various speech organs. You learn how to make most of the common speech sounds and how to recognize them when you hear them. Also you learn how to describe and classify them.

If you are dealing with a well-known language, phonetics helps you to learn its sounds more quickly and to produce them more accurately. If you come in contact with an unwritten language, it enables you to distinguish the sounds it uses and to reproduce them. It also gives you an accurate way of writing down words and phrases so you can use them later and teach them to others.

Most missionaries will not really need more than the course in phonetics. But those who are going to give much of their time to linguistic work on the field, especially those who reduce languages to writing and translate the Bible, will need much more. Without doubt the most useful training of this sort for missionary candidates is that provided by the Summer Institute of Linguistics (Camp Wycliffe). You can take the foundational course in one summer session of a little less than three months of intensive work.

A second type of training quite generally needed is in the line of medicine. That is, it is medical instruction for the average missionary, the one who does not intend to be a doctor or a nurse.

Every missionary ought to know the elementary things about anatomy and physiology, hygiene, first aid and care of the sick. Competent medical help in many fields is still all too little, and too widely scattered, to take care of all the needs. The missionary ought to know at least how to care for himself and his family in ordinary circumstances, and he ought to know how to care for an emergency until he can get a doctor.

Another thing. In some cases, where the law permits, the non-medical missionary can treat illnesses among the people as far as his knowledge and ability go. He knows he is not a doctor. But when no doctor can be had, he does what he can. The need for this medical work by non-medical missionaries is getting less and less. There are many more fully trained doctors than there used to be, both missionary and native. But there are still some places where the need is likely to continue for some years.

Just how much medical training is advisable for the general missionary? This is a matter on which there is no general agreement. Too much depends on the particular field, the government restrictions, and even the personality of the missionary. The amount of training that might prove very useful to one missionary might even be dangerous for another with less discretion. But everyone ought to get instruction in the basic subjects we mentioned above: anatomy and physiology, hygiene, first aid and care of the sick. For tropical lands it is good to know something about the more common tropical diseases and how to treat them.

A third type of training, which is even more generally needed, is training in teaching. We are not talking here about those who are going to give full time to teaching. Every missionary is a teacher. No matter what his special ministry may be, he is usually called on to do some teaching. He may be teaching printing, or nursing, or carpentry; or he may be teaching the Bible and theology. But whatever his ministry, teaching is a part of it. He is never just a workman. He is one who inspires and teaches others to do what he does.

So each missionary ought to take some training in the principles of teaching. His training doesn't have to be as complete as that of the professional teacher, but it should give him a grasp of the fundamentals. Besides, he ought to get some experience in teaching. If he can get it under the direction of a skilled teacher, so much the better. But if not, he ought to get the experience of teaching, anyway.

For a fourth type of general preparation we are going to mention bookkeeping and business management. It may amaze some that these subjects are considered important for most missionaries. Yet mission leaders have been urging the matter for many years. We are not concerned here about the general accounts and business affairs of the whole mission. For such things the mission can usually get someone with special training and experience.

But every mission station has its own accounts to keep and business affairs to handle. Building, repairing, hiring laborers of all sorts require some ability in business affairs and accounts. Schools, Bible institutes, and even "bush" schools make the same demands. And so do such things as hospitals, printing plants, colportage work and even Bible conferences. Many a mission treasurer has groaned over the seeming inability of some missionaries to keep simple accounts and make intelligible financial reports.

What is needed for the individual missionary is not a complete business course, though that has its value. But he does need the principles of bookkeeping. He can take that in high school and in some Bible institutes. And he ought to have some business experience. Training in business management of the simple sort the missionary needs is not so available as bookkeeping. But if he can't get a regular course in it, he will usually find that a little business experience is a great asset.

SPECIALIZATION

Specialization is the order of the day in our American civilization. Men concentrate their studies not just on one field of knowledge, but on a fragment of one portion of that field.

Such intensive work has produced great results in the field of the physical sciences. Many people don't see why it wouldn't do just as well in the mission field.

Perhaps it might. That is, if the missions had enough money to employ the large staff of specialists they would need in any one field. And if there were enough trained specialists volunteering for the work. And if people didn't insist on looking at themselves as individuals instead of a collection of characteristics, and at the Gospel as a whole Gospel for a whole man. But these conditions don't exist.

Complete specialization in missions is out of the question. There are some specialists, some who give their whole time to just one phase of the work. But the majority of missionaries have to be ready to take on various kinds of work. They are not jacks-of-all-trades, but they can't limit themselves to just one, either. There is so much to be done and so few to do it that sometimes the missionaries pray, "Lord, deliver us from the specialist, the fellow who won't do whatever needs to be done!"

Yet because specialization is normal and valuable, there has always been some of it in missions. Every missionary has some things that he does better than others, some interests that attract him more than others. No matter to what job he is assigned, he will always find time and place for his special interest. Also, there have always been certain types of work that demanded the full-time services of specially trained workers. And present conditions have increased that need for specialization.

So if you want to be a missionary, keep these things in mind. First, most missionaries have to do more things than the one they like to do most. Second, if you have real talent and training in a line that is useful to the work, sooner or later you will have a chance to make use of your specialty. Third, in some specialized fields your chances to be used full time are quite broad, while in others they may be very limited.

Medical work more and more calls for the fully trained, full-time doctor or nurse. There are still a few places where the non-medical missionary can give some medical help, as we said before, but the number is rapidly decreasing. On the other hand, the demand for well-trained missionary doctors always exceeds the supply. Nurses, too, are generally needed. But not in all fields. There are some fields where foreign doctors are not allowed to practice. There are others where the local doctors can meet most of the need. So the medical missionary candidate has to expect some limitation in his choice of field. He may not get to go to the place he first chooses.

Teaching is another specialized field that often calls for the full-time services of trained men and women. There are many kinds of teaching, and not all are carried on in any one field or mission. The teaching and directing of primary schools is of course the most common, if we don't count the Bible schools. Teaching on the high school and college level offers fewer opportunities, but the supply of teachers is still short of the demand.

Printing is carried on by many separate missions as well as by several missions working together. It usually calls for a full-time printer, who will also train and supervise native help. Trained men are very important in this work, and they are usually in demand. But you may have less choice of field than in the case of doctors and teachers.

As we get into other technical fields, we find the opportunities even more limited. Full-time builders are needed, but only by the larger missions. The same is true of business managers. Laboratory technicians can be used where there are hospitals. Airplane pilots usually need to double as mechanics. They can be used in a limited number of fields where special needs call for missionary aviation.

Radio technicians are needed by the few missionary radio stations. They are also needed where a mission has set up a short-wave communications system between its stations. Agricultural experts are very useful in some fields, as well as teachers of the crafts. And there are other useful specialties too many to mention. You can see, though, that full-time service in any one of these specialties may be limited to certain fields and missions.

There is another type of specialization that we ought to deal with. It is the type that we can best illustrate by speaking of literary work. Very rarely does a mission send out a new missionary with the express purpose of doing literary work in another language. Instead, when anyone is set aside for this ministry, he is usually a veteran missionary.

The reason is simple. Training in the United States is for an English-speaking American public. It is good as far as it goes. But it usually takes some years for any man to learn another language well enough to produce a literature in it. Besides, the missionary doesn't have to learn just the language. He has to learn the people. He has to know what needs to be written and how. He needs to know how the people think, what the background is for their beliefs and actions. He needs to write, insofar as he can, from their point of view. This calls for experience in the land and with the people. There are other specialties like this, too, that are best developed on the field.

It is a weakness in most of our courses of preparation that so many of the students have no other purpose than just "to be a missionary." If we ask, "What kind of missionary?" their answers are very vague.

To be well prepared, a missionary candidate should find out as soon as possible in what kind of service the Lord can best use him. He may have major and minor interests, but he does need to have objectives. He needs to realize that evangelism is itself a specialty and that it takes special preparation. How can he say that he expects to be an evangelistic missionary if he hasn't learned to do personal evangelism? Or hasn't learned to preach in his own tongue? Or isn't on familiar terms with the Gospel message? Or shrinks from contact with new people?

And if the prospective missionary wants to be used in one of these other ways, he should definitely prepare himself for that service to the best of his ability.

Medical missionaries need to be fully qualified to practice in this country before they are sent abroad. Teachers usually need to be certified at home. In addition, for both of them there may be other requirements in the field to which they are going. They would both have to take courses in Belgium, for example, before going to the Belgian Congo.

And for each one of the technical specialties the missionary should get the best of training. Those who handle airplanes, for instance, need more than a private pilot's license. A sound aviation program calls for a pilot with at least a commercial license, and usually a license in aircraft and engine maintenance.

We can't go further into the matter of specialized preparation. But we do need to remind ourselves again that training in these specialties doesn't exempt a candidate from the basic preparation required of all missionaries. They are missionaries, too. They must be motivated by the same spirit as the evangelistic missionaries. Otherwise the work will suffer. Experience has shown us that each new worker added, if he is not a real missionary, dilutes the spiritual effectiveness of the work. We need specialists, but *missionary* specialists.

CHAPTER XVI

MISSION BOARDS

WHY MISSION BOARDS?

MOST PEOPLE TODAY accept the existence of mission boards without any question. They are quite the normal thing in missions. They have certain rather definite duties to perform, and they have clearly been used in the expansion of the missionary enterprise.

However, there are a number of sincere and devout Christians, including some missionaries, who are opposed to mission boards. Some base their opposition on doctrinal grounds, claiming that such organizations are not Scriptural. Others are governed more by their personal situation and interests. Some have used such catch-phrases as "It is better to have a Rock under your feet than a board behind your back." As if you couldn't have both!

We can state the opposition on Scriptural grounds quite simply. Generally those who hold this position are opposed to most formal organization in the church. They take it for granted that the New Testament gives us a complete and detailed pattern of all that a Christian church ought to be and do. This includes the methods by which we are to carry on missionary work. We should have no other organization than what we find in the pages of the New Testament. And of course we find no mission boards there.

We respect the sincere faith and earnest zeal of those who

hold this view. Some of them have done very good missionary work. Yet they represent the view of only a small minority of all earnest Christians. And most of us don't find in the Scriptures themselves any claim to such finality in matters of organization and methods. In doctrine, yes. The New Testament does present Jesus Christ as God's final and complete revelation. It pronounces an anathema on all who would preach any other Gospel than what it presents. But we think it is a mistake to extend those claims of finality in doctrine to matters of organization.

In fact, the New Testament itself does not give a unified picture of organization and procedure. What it does give us is a picture of development under the guidance of the Holy Spirit, a developing organization to meet the needs as they arose.

Christ left only the nucleus of an organization in the eleven apostles. After His ascension they chose another to complete the original number of Twelve. The church in Jerusalem grew so fast that soon they had to create the office of deacon to take proper care of needy members.

We don't know when the elders in Jerusalem were first chosen, or why. But we can see the similarity to the Jewish synagogue with which they were familiar. We can also see the need for such officers when the apostles themselves began to die off or to leave for other fields. When Barnabas and Paul started the first churches in Asia Minor, they reversed the procedure. They appointed elders first, since the apostles didn't stay with the churches. The deacons seem to have come later as they were needed.

Mission boards in their modern sense don't appear in the New Testament. In fact, we have had them for only a little over a century and a half. But the basic principle on which they are organized agrees fully with New Testament teaching.

As we stated before, Christ laid the responsibility for carrying out His Great Commission on the church as a whole, as well as on individuals. And clearly the New Testament church recognized that responsibility, even though it didn't see just how far it was to go.

So when Philip started the work in Samaria, the church at Jerusalem sent an official delegation to confirm it. When Peter preached to Cornelius, his conduct was officially reviewed by the church. The decision in that case was to be the deciding factor in their approval of the work of Barnabas and Paul, years later. When the church began in Antioch, the church sent Barnabas to confirm the believers in their faith. And when Barnabas and Saul started on their first missionary tour, it was the church at Antioch that sent them forth, by direction of the Holy Spirit. They also reported to the church there when they returned.

But the church did not take on financial responsibility for any of its missionaries. That is a very modern development. Neither did it dictate where they were to go, nor how they were to carry on the work. These men were pioneers, and there was no one able to instruct them. Later on, Paul himself does give some very definite instructions to the younger missionaries, Timothy and Titus. Also, though the church at Antioch didn't provide their financial needs, other churches did send help to them on various occasions. And of course, as happens in some places today, the people to whom they ministered would often see that they had food and shelter.

The modern mission board is intended to represent the church in the carrying out of its missionary task. It is formed within the church and is the servant of the church. Its constitution and practices reflect the church that it represents. And since there are a number of different denominations, their boards may have different practices. The funds that the mission board has to use are the gifts of the members of the church. So it is responsible to the church for the handling of them.

Of course there are a number of boards that are not denominational. But they are still representative. They represent a large and growing number of independent churches, plus many groups and individuals within the denominations, people who for one reason or another are interested in their work. These boards are not so immediately responsible to their supporters, but the work depends on keeping their interest and support. In fact, this support is more spontaneous and less regular than that of the denominations, so the mission is apt to be more sensitive to the attitudes of its supporters. One such independent board finally developed its own denomination in the United States.

We need mission boards for the effective, systematic spread of the Gospel, just as the Jerusalem church needed deacons for the fair, systematic distribution of material help to needy believers. It can't be done on an "every-man-for-himself" basis. It is the church's business, and that means co-operation. And co-operation calls for some sort of organization.

Take, for example, the handling of the church's gifts for missions. In a large mission, operating in several fields, this is a big job. It isn't just a matter of sending a salary to each missionary in the field. That would be simple, even if you had to vary the salary according to the size of each family. But there are other things to consider. Living costs are different in every field, and they often change rapidly. Money exchange rates are always changing. The American dollar that will get you five dollars in one country will get only sixty cents in another. The board takes this into account.

Then there are expenses for building, for running schools and hospitals, for printing, for travel, for a multitude of other things that are needed to carry on the mission. And besides, the churches don't give with regularity. Giving reaches its peak just before the end of the year, partly because of Christmas but even more because of the income tax deadline. On the other hand, the summer months are very slim. Business is slack, church attendance is off, and many people are spending their money on vacations instead of missions. Yet the missionary needs the same support in the summer as in the winter. The board plans the handling of funds to take care of these matters.

We need the mission boards also to represent the work at home. If missions is the church's job, if the churches are to support the work spiritually and financially, they must have reports on how it is going. Interest has to be fed by information.

It is entirely possible for the missionaries themselves to keep up a certain amount of interest by personal letters and by their visits while on furlough. That is good, but it is not enough. Most churches don't have any personal touch with more than one or two missionaries, if at all. Then too, most missionaries are not well acquainted with the work outside their own stations. Their letters and their talks deal mostly with their own personal experiences.

Only the mission board is in a position to view the whole field and present a balanced picture of progress and needs. It usually tries to do this through the mission magazine, or through visits to the churches by secretaries and others. Sometimes it sponsors the taking of motion pictures or slides that can be shown in the churches to represent the whole work. Or it helps promote missionary education in the churches, providing the needed plans and literature. Or it plans and conducts missionary conferences.

Of course mission boards are needed to secure, examine and counsel missionary candidates. The local church is not in a position to do this. It may know the candidate and his spiritual fitness, but it doesn't know the field and its needs.

Then when the new missionary is ready to leave for the field, he needs counsel and help in purchasing, shipping, getting transportation, etc. Here, too, the mission board is needed. And there are many other ways in which it proves its value.

We have said that mission boards are usually taken for granted. But there are many who criticize them without good ground because they think they are too expensive for the work they do.

Several years ago a certain writer published the claim that one denomination was spending 87 per cent of its missionary income on overhead expenses. He justified this claim on the ground that each missionary got a salary of $1000 per year, and that when you multiplied that by the number of missionaries it only accounted for 13 per cent of the total expenditures. All the rest, he concluded, was overhead.

This was far from true. The salary of the individual missionary was indeed $1000. But that didn't include rent, medical allowances, group insurance, pension payments, and emergency payments in certain critical areas. It didn't even include allowances for the children. The actual average support for each missionary that year came to more than $2000.

But this is not all. Missionaries had to be transported to and from the field. They had to travel on the field. They had to be equipped for their work. They had to be provided with literature. Equipment and supplies for hospitals and dispensaries were expensive. Seminaries, Bible schools and schools of other types took money. As a matter of fact, the board's financial report for that year showed less than 9 per cent spent at home, while more than 91 cents out of every dollar contributed was spent on the field.

It may be that some boards are not as economical as they should be. But it is doubtful whether any business concern doing business abroad is getting by with as low a percentage of overhead as the most extravagant mission board.

CHAPTER XVII

MISSION BOARDS (*Continued*)

Types of Mission Boards

M OST MISSION BOARDS may be divided into two general types: denominational and independent. We shall talk about the denominational boards first. Even though their work in recent years has not been growing as rapidly as that of the independent boards, and in many cases has declined, it still represents the greater part of Protestant missionary effort.

In the United States today the denominational mission board is usually set up by the denomination and is under the control of the denomination. It is not independent of the churches but is considered to be the organization through which the churches carry on their missionary work. It is the denomination at work for missions.

Also in the United States it is usual for each denomination to have only one board of foreign missions; or, in some of the larger denominations, a general board and a women's board. These boards are under the control of the governing body of the denomination and they make their reports to it.

Denominational missions of course depend on the churches of their denomination to provide both the funds and the manpower for their missionary work. Candidates are expected to belong to churches of the denomination. There are very few exceptions.

The larger denominational boards often have work in a number of different fields. Although they do set up a field organization in each of these places, the board at home has the over-all supervision and has final authority. In earlier days the missionaries often had reason to criticize the boards because they didn't understand the situation on the field. Today this is not nearly so true. The boards often appoint experienced missionaries as secretaries and have them visit the fields periodically to keep in touch with what is going on.

Even though each church in a denomination may be given a quota for its missionary giving, the offerings in the churches are still voluntary. The board may make an appeal for money, but that is as far as it can go. Its income depends on the generosity of the members of the churches. It draws up its annual budget and makes its plans on the basis of what it estimates will be the probable giving during the year.

When the board appoints a missionary, it puts him on a regular salary. This salary is always small, and it has no relation to the value of his work. Missionary salaries are not competitive. Perhaps they ought rather to be called living allowances. The amount varies from field to field according to the cost of living. It is proportionately more for those who have children, since it is based on needs instead of merit. And because it is only intended to cover the needs of the missionary and his family, the mission does not usually care to appoint missionaries who have dependent relatives or unpaid debts. They wouldn't be able to meet these extra obligations.

One problem in mission financing has always been hard to solve. People just don't like to give to mission boards. Whatever the reason, many of them prefer to give to individual missionaries or to special projects. This has forced missions to adopt various plans of "personalized giving."

Generally the idea is that one or more churches may take on the support of a missionary and consider him their missionary. The missionary then keeps in touch with his supporting church and, if it is not his own home church, he is expected to visit it when he is home on furlough. The amount of his allowance is set by the board in every case, but it is provided by a specific church.

The independent missions are so called because they are not under the control of a church or denomination. They usually have a self-perpetuating board of directors. That is, if one member of the board resigns or dies, the others elect a man to take his place. In many cases the missionaries themselves are not considered employees of the mission but members of it, having a voice in all its affairs. Sometimes churches and individuals who donate to the mission more than a stated amount per year are considered members with a right to vote in the annual meeting.

A large part of the independent missions, though not all, are called faith missions. They got this name, not because they claimed to have more faith than others, but because of their financial principles. They make it a rule not to make any direct appeal for funds except to God alone. They believe He will move upon the hearts of Christians to give for any work that is truly of Him. Of course their missionaries can't be assured of any stated salary. They have to look to the Lord to send in what they need. Such a plan sounds utterly visionary. But it works. In fact, it has proved very successful in many missions.

The independent missions get their support from the growing number of independent churches in the homeland as well as from many people and even churches within the denominations. Some simply prefer the independent missions to their denominational missions. Others have enough interest to make these donations above and beyond what their quota is in the denomination. Denominational stalwarts don't like the idea. They do their best to oblige the people to give all their gifts just to the denomination. But they usually find that you can't control free-will giving.

Some of the independent missions, especially among the Baptists, are really denominational in character. They are not under the control of the denomination, and sometimes they adopt the faith principle of financing, but in other ways they are denominational. If they are Baptist, all the members of the mission have to be Baptist; candidates are told that they must be Baptist "by principle, not for convenience"; and the churches they establish on the field are Baptist both in name and in practice.

But perhaps the largest part of the independent missions are interdenominational faith missions. That is, their membership and support comes from different evangelical denominations as well as from the independent churches. They are conservative in theology. They usually hold to a brief doctrinal statement that covers the fundamentals of the faith but omits some of the controversial points that have separated the denominations. On this basis they welcome Presbyterians, Methodists, Baptists, Congregationalists and many others into their fellowship.

The first of these interdenominational missions, and the one that has served as a pattern for many others, is the China Inland Mission. It was founded in England in 1865 by Dr. J. Hudson Taylor. Taylor had spent several years in China as a missionary and then returned home broken in health. But he had a continuing passion for the conversion of the Chinese people.

Without going into details, these are the facts that led to the starting of the mission. Taylor was burdened for the vast interior of China. But it was not really open at the time. Besides, the missions already in China did not believe they could take on any more responsibilities than what they already had. To reach the interior a new mission would be needed. But it wouldn't have any denomination to sponsor it.

Now Taylor in his experience had come to several conclusions. One was the conviction that "God's work done in God's way will not lack God's supply." If this was true, then it would be wrong to go into debt. Why should we try to borrow from men what God has seen fit to withhold? Taylor was also sure that evangelism was the great need of inland China. For that purpose it was not necessary to insist on missionaries who had all the educational preparation usually required. He believed the mission boards were passing over many who might prove very useful missionaries.

But while Taylor had learned to trust God for his own needs without making appeals to men, it would be different to form a mission on that basis. What if he should get young people out to China, and then the funds should fail? Could he carry such a responsibility? His reluctance was not overcome until he came to realize that if God was moving him to start the mission, the responsibility was God's, not his. In that confidence he went ahead.

In the missions that have followed the example of the China Inland Mission, the following principles are generally observed:

(1) No solicitation of funds or missionaries is permitted.

(2) No debts are allowed.

(3) No salary is guaranteed.

(4) Missionary candidates from any evangelical denomination are acceptable.

(5) Evangelistic work is to have first place.

Even though they hold to the faith principle in financing, not all the faith missions use the same plan. There is room for a great deal of diversity. However, in general two main plans, with modifications, seem to stand out.

First is the pooling plan. Under this plan all gifts for missionary support are put into one common fund, or pool. When the regular distribution is made, usually once a month, each missionary gets his share. Single missionaries in the same field all get the same amount. Married missionaries get a larger amount, depending on the number of children they have. There are other details, but the principle is that of share and share alike.

The missions usually set up some definite amount as an objective, an amount that they think will cover the missionary's needs. The larger missions can foretell with reasonable accuracy their probable receipts, so they draw up a budget on that basis.

The pooling plan has several advantages. It avoids inequalities among the missionaries, since all share alike. The missionary with a thrilling story to tell gets no more than the one whose service is more humdrum but perhaps just as valuable. Even if people at home try to by-pass the rule and send their gifts directly to the missionary, it makes no difference. He has to report these direct receipts, and they are counted in the common pool and deducted from his next remittance. Most missions do, however, permit bona fide gifts for such things as birthdays, Christmas, a new baby, etc., without their entering into the pool.

The plan impresses upon the missionary the need of praying for the needs of the whole mission and not just his own. When one profits, all profit; when one gets a short remittance, they are all short. No one is ever left completely without support, even if his supporting church drops him. This tends to greater unity in the mission and exalts the mission above the individual missionary.

But the plan also has some weaknesses. It has happened that missions have sent to the field more missionaries than they could support properly. Then all the missionaries suffered hardship. (Though it should be said to the credit of the missionaries that they didn't complain.) But the greatest weakness is in the attitude of the donors at home. There are many who insist that they want their gifts to go wholly to the missionary they are supporting. They don't want them pooled.

No amount of explanation will satisfy them. If the missionary doesn't get just what they send, then they won't send.

That is what has given rise to the second plan, the individual support plan. Under this plan the individual missionary gets exactly whatever his friends and supporters give for him. It may be much or little. But it must be specified for him. The mission will provide information about the amount he should have to be properly supported, but it doesn't take responsibility for his support.

However, it does make this provision. All unspecified gifts to the mission are put into a general fund. This fund is meant to cover all expenses except the missionary's personal support. If the missionary does not get enough personal support for his needs, the mission may add to his income from the general fund, provided there is enough money to do so.

The individual support plan also has some advantages. It capitalizes on the desire of so many donors to give to individual missionaries. And it makes a close bond between them and the missionary they support. It also spurs the missionary to keep in touch with the people who support him. He can't count on being carried along by what the others are able to do.

But it also has its weaknesses. Gifts to the general fund are usually insufficient. Too many people prefer to give to a person rather than to the mission. Then some missionaries get better support than others whose work is equally valuable. They may have more friends or may be better at inspiring interest through their talks and letters. And because the worker is more prominent than the work, the sense of unity in the mission is weakened.

The picture we have given of these two plans is not complete. We have oversimplified it. What most missions do is use one or another of the basic plans with modifications. This has become more and more true of those that use the individual support plan.

Today it is not at all uncommon for such a mission to expect a missionary to get both personal and service support. That is, a certain part of the funds donated for him is designated as service support. This money is to cover services rendered by the mission on behalf of the missionary, but which he does not personally pay. It may include such things as the cost of sending his money to him, his rent, and his share in any number of other expenditures for his benefit. This relieves some of the pressure on the usually depleted general fund.

Each mission is willing to explain its plan of financing to a donor or candidate on request.

CHAPTER XVIII

HOW TO CHOOSE A MISSION

To MANY PEOPLE the choice of a mission is no problem at all. They are members of one of our Protestant denominations. They either have a general call or are called to a specific field in which their denomination is working. And they see no reason why they should not be accepted and work in harmony with their denominational board.

There are advantages in working with the mission of your own denomination. As a missionary it makes you feel that you represent not just the church to which you belong but the whole denomination. Other churches besides your own are presumably interested in your work.

In addition, you work on the field with other missionaries who come from churches like your own. Their doctrinal views are largely the same. The churches they have started use an organization you are familiar with. And in other ways you are made to feel at home. Sometimes, too, you will find in the mission an organizational and financial stability that are not always present in the independent missions.

But for some, even in the denominations, the matter is not that simple. There are reasons why they hesitate to ask for appointment under the denominational board. The board doesn't always appreciate those reasons, but they are very real to the missionary volunteer.

One of the main reasons is theological modernism. Not in

the official statements of belief. There are probably none of our denominations that have adopted officially modernistic creeds. So there are many churches that have not followed the modernistic trend and are considered decidedly conservative in their denomination. It is also true that there are many members of modernistic churches who are not in sympathy with their modernism but have not yet come to the place of leaving them.

Conditions are not the same in all denominations. Neither are they the same in all mission fields of any one denomination. But it is not at all uncommon to have a young person say, "I would prefer not to serve under my denominational board; it is too modernistic."

We have mentioned that the board often doesn't appreciate this viewpoint. It says that it hasn't any objection to the candidate's holding to his more conservative beliefs if he wants to. It can't understand why he won't be just as tolerant of the beliefs of others.

But it is more than a matter of personal viewpoints. It is a matter of basic principles. We can be tolerant of others' beliefs if the differences are not important to us. We can't be so tolerant if we believe they are basic issues.

In such a case the candidate's hesitation is perfectly proper. If the missionaries themselves are not agreed on their message, how can their mission be successful? And if a missionary cannot have spiritual fellowship with the other missionaries, how can he stand the strain of missionary life and give good service?

There are others who do not want to work with their denominational boards because they believe they have been called to another field or type of ministry than the ones in which their board is engaged. Sometimes this happens when the board's ministry is almost wholly institutional and not evangelistic. For it is true that in some of the major denominational missions evangelism holds a very minor place.

Then there are some who might like to work with their denomination but can't meet the requirements, especially in educational preparation. And there are actually quite a few young people who have come to dislike the narrow denominationalism of their churches and would like to serve in a broader fellowship.

Add to these the members of the many independent churches, and members of denominations too small to support an extensive missionary work of their own, and we have a large group of young people who want to know how to choose a mission board. Their choice is made doubly hard because many of the independent missions work in only one field, so that the choice of a mission is also the choice of a field.

If the young volunteer is sure of his field, the following suggestions will be helpful:

(1) Find out what boards are in that field.

(2) Get all the information you can about the missions there and the work they are doing.

(3) Write to those with which you might be interested in serving. Tell them of your interest and ask for more information about the mission, its organization, principles, requirements, etc. Don't fail to tell them also something about yourself, so they can tell whether to encourage you.

(4) If possible, have personal interviews with mission representatives and individual missionaries.

(5) Above all, and through all, wait upon the Lord for guidance.

There may be a special divine call to a certain work. But at any rate there should be a whole-hearted conviction that the mission you choose is where God wants you.

If the prospective missionary is not sure of his field, he may do one of two things. He may wait until the Lord shows him the field. Or he may choose a mission on its own merits without reference to the field, under God's guidance.

This latter course of action is usually the better. We have already seen that a missionary call is not necessarily associated with any particular field of service. It is quite a common thing for zealous young missionary volunteers to be uncertain about their precise fields. If they waited to be sure of the field before approaching a mission, many would never reach any field.

The relative unimportance of knowing the exact field is seen in the fact that many a missionary today is serving successfully in a different field from the one he first had in mind. In fact, hundreds of missionaries have been transferred from one field to another without losing any of their effectiveness. See where the China missionaries are today.

Much more important is the mission board. A real missionary is seldom disappointed in his field after he gets there. But there are all too many occasions when he becomes disappointed in the mission with which he is working. It is amazing how little attention many pay to these things. As if the people you work with in the Lord's service were always easy to get along with and never succumbed to temptation!

There are a number of specific things about a mission that every candidate ought to find out if he can. We shall list some of them here in the form of questions, not necessarily in the order of importance.

(1) Doctrinal standards

What is the theological position of the mission and its missionaries? It is easy to get the answer to this question. The mission usually has an official doctrinal statement that it publishes from time to time in its magazine. If not, it will gladly send it to you. Do you agree with it fully? If you have any hesitation, move slowly. Of course if you are not in full sympathy with what it stands for, the mission probably wouldn't accept your application anyway.

(2) Finances

Are the mission accounts regularly audited? Is the audit

published so that anyone may examine it? For most people it makes dull reading, but you can well be suspicious of any mission that doesn't publish such a statement.

What plan of missionary support is used: pooling, individual support, or some modification? You may not have any preference, but you ought to know which is used.

Are the missionaries well cared for? This is not always easy to find out. But it might influence your decision, especially under the pooling plan.

(3) Origin and aims

How and why did the mission start? If it is a split off from another group, why? If the reason was good and sound, the mission itself will not hesitate to tell about it. If it does hesitate, be careful.

Is the mission meeting a real need? That is, is it performing a service that is badly needed and that no other group could do? Or is it in the same area with other good missions and competing with them? There is more of this than the people at home realize. It may be best to get this information from sources outside the mission itself.

(4) Organization and methods

Young people themselves are not often the best judges in this matter. Yet they should not be so willfully blind as the pastor who wrote us for information about a certain questionable mission. He said, "Please tell me about its doctrinal position and its financial honesty; I am not interested in its methods."

Is the control in the hands of one or two individuals? In very small missions this may not be significant, but a personal or family dictatorship never works out well. Incorporation doesn't mean a thing in this regard; it has to do only with the conduct of financial affairs.

On the other hand, it is just as dangerous for the individual missionary to have too much independence. There needs to be authority which is recognized and obeyed.

Who is on the governing board of the mission? Who sponsors its work? Don't be misled by so-called "councils of reference." These are just lists of men who have been persuaded to allow their names to be used to recommend the mission. They may know something about its affairs, but just as often they don't. They are window-dressing. They have no authority in the mission itself.

(5) Fellowship

Missionary relationships on the field are so close that it is important to have a good basis for real fellowship. A fellowship that might be very enjoyable to one might not suit another at all. For this reason it is good to have an opportunity to get acquainted with some of the missionaries before going to the field.

Often after meeting the leaders of the work you may ask yourself this question, "Are these the kind of leaders I would be glad to follow, people who would inspire me to my best service for the Lord?"

Another practical question. Are the other missionaries of your nationality and culture? It is not easy to be a foreigner in a foreign land and at the same time feel that you are a foreigner in the mission. Some of us can find congenial service with those of another nationality; but we need to face the fact that the adjustment is more than many are able to make with real success. We ought to, but we don't.

(6) Reputation

Does the mission have a good name among other missions? Remember, other missions on the field are in a better position to judge of the value of a work than are any of the people in the homeland. And they are usually inclined to be charitable in their judgments. One or two might possibly give a bad report through jealousy; but if several agree in such a report it is best to be wary.

You can judge the interdenominational missions on this point by seeing whether they are members of the Interdenominational Foreign Mission Association of North America (IFMA). Only missions of good reputation are accepted into this association. They must also be interdenominational missions, evangelical in their theology, follow the faith principle of missionary operation, and publish an annual audit of their accounts. Missions in the association have a total missionary force of well over five thousand missionaries.

(7) Missionary turnover

Do the missionaries generally stay with the mission? Allow for some who have to leave the field because of illness or some other good reason. But does the number of those who leave the mission in a comparatively short time seem unreasonably high? Do they go back for a second, third and other terms of service? An unusually high turnover means there is something wrong, regardless of the reasons the missionaries may give for their leaving.

Although the suggestions we have just made are useful, they will not settle the question for you. The decision is yours. There are some factors in the decision that are known only to you and God. Be frank with Him, and let Him lead you to the best choice.

CHAPTER XIX

INDEPENDENT MISSIONARIES

ON THE FRINGE of the missionary movement are a great many independent missionaries. They are called independent missionaries because they are not connected with any organized missionary society. Each one carries on his work independent of anyone else, and usually independent of any authority in the homeland.

There are a number of reasons for these independent missionaries. A large part of them originally went to the field under some organized society. Then, for one reason or another, they withdrew from the society but decided to keep on working in the field. Some of them are individuals who find it hard to work in harmony with others, or to submit to authority. In other cases their mission itself was at least partly at fault. But in any case they are missionaries who don't join another society but go on working alone.

There are others who go to the field independently because they haven't found a mission that would accept them. It may be a matter of health, or age, or some other lack in their qualifications. But when the regular missions turn them down, they somehow find a way of getting enough financial support to go to the field on their own.

A third group are those who believe they have a call to a specific field but can't find a satisfactory mission in that field. There may be some extremists among them who are very hard to please, or even some who don't want to be limited by authority over them. But often their argument is perfectly valid that there is no suitable mission for them in that particular field.

A last group, and one that we are going to deal with separately, is what are commonly called nonprofessional missionaries. Some of them are Christians whom circumstances have taken to other lands, where they do what they can in a missionary way. Others are earnest believers who have deliberately chosen to go to foreign countries to practice their trade or profession in order that they may also do some missionary work. They support themselves by their earnings, try to live a consistent Christian life, and devote their spare time to witnessing for Christ.

The two groups to which we are going to give most of our attention are the second and third. These are the ones who deliberately choose to go to the field independent of any mission society and give their full time to the work. They are constantly approaching missionary counselors, explaining what they want to do and then asking, "Would you advise me to go out independently?"

I have never yet heard of an experienced missionary who answered *yes* to such a question. He will usually give a number of reasons why such a course is very unwise. But he is often too polite to mention two basic questions that the inquirer ought to face.

The first is this, "If the regular missions have turned you down, are you really fit for missionary service?" The missions do sometimes make mistakes. Sometimes they turn down a candidate who would make a good missionary. More often they accept one who should not be accepted. But they are less liable to mistakes than is any individual. Before going ahead, make doubly sure that it is really the mission that is making the mistake and not you. Remember that if you couldn't succeed in the mission you will stand even less chance independently.

The second question is for those who can't find a satisfactory mission in their chosen field. "Just why are you so sure that you should go to that field and not to any other?" Sometimes the candidate speaks quite confidently of a call. And of course if it is God's calling none of us would want to stand in the way. But there are so many imitations of the call of God. There are so many young people who feel attracted to certain fields without knowing a thing about the real situation and needs there. It is the fields that attract them, not needy human beings. Be sure it is God's call and not the echo of your own desires.

Now there may be an overpowering reason or a distinct call that will lead a missionary into independent work. But before he decides to undertake it, and before any local church decides to sponsor any such activity, they should both know some of the handicaps that will have to be faced.

First of all, there are some fields today into which no missionary can gain an entrance unless he comes as the representative of a recognized society. This is not because the government discriminates against one form of Christianity or another. It is simply that it has found it much better to deal with responsible organizations than with every Tom, Dick and Harry.

Second, just where are you going and what is the need there? When a well-organized board decides to open a new field, it doesn't blindly plunge into it. First of all it makes a careful survey to find out what the needs are. It consults with other missions in the field so as not to duplicate what they are doing. In the light of these studies it plans its occupation.

The independent missionary almost never does this. His choice of a location is largely a hit-or-miss proposition. And more often than not he hits on a place where he comes into competition with other missions. But he seldom mentions it in his letters home.

Of course there are great needs in most fields. So if the independent missionary will work in co-operation with others, letting his work supplement theirs, he can often find a niche where he can make a real contribution. He may even, after a time, be accepted into the ranks of the mission. It has happened. But most independent missionaries are intent on starting a work all of their own, be it ever so tiny and evanescent.

A serious practical difficulty that faces the independent missionary from the beginning is his lack of experienced counsel. He doesn't know what kind nor how much of an outfit to take with him. He can easily arrange transportation in normal times to the principal ports or airports; but the newcomer without help who tries to proceed inland soon finds himself at the mercy of any glib swindler with a smattering of English. For of course he doesn't know the language of the country, and he is not familiar with its currency nor the legitimate prices. Not knowing where to find lodging, he usually takes advantage of the hospitality of some other missionary. (I have often admired the long-suffering generosity of missionaries in the major cities. How often they are imposed on!) At every step in his inexperience he makes unnecessary blunders from which the counsel of others could have saved him.

And what work is he going to do? Supposing he has somehow learned the language, and found or built a suitable house, and learned how to get along in the land, what will his ministry be? At home he would be called to the pastorate of a church already established and would find that a big enough job for one man. Here he can't possibly do all that needs to be done.

There's the literature, for example. Even supposing the Bible has already been translated into the language of his people, where is he going to get the other Christian literature —the Sunday school lessons, the devotional books, the Christian magazines—that are so helpful to the pastor at home? And who will teach his teachers? Who will train his young people for Christian service? Missionary work is just too big for any one person. It calls for co-operation.

And even as the work is too big for the independent missionary working alone, so the independent church coming from his ministry is too small for satisfactory Christian fellowship and service. We often see this in the experience of the young people. When the time comes to marry, they are told that they should marry in the church. Yet their own church fellowship is so limited that they have little choice. The result is that many marry outside the church and are lost to it. And who has ever attended a conference of churches on the mission field and has not been thrilled at the joy of some of the believers when they see that their small congregation is a part of a much larger fellowship!

But the final and often the greatest test of the work of the independent missionary comes when he must leave that work. It may be for furlough; it may be permanently. Furlough always is a problem. It is a problem even when someone else can fill in for the missionary on furlough. But in the organized mission the problem is minimized. Usually another missionary is assigned to relieve the one on furlough. Or if not, the mission makes some other provision to take care of the work while he is away. It is not likely to be dropped.

The independent missionary has only one choice. Either he must stay on at the risk of a complete breakdown in health, or he must abandon the work for the time of furlough at the risk of a breakdown in the work. Whichever he does, the work is likely to suffer.

Sometimes young people have objected, "But he ought to have a national worker prepared to take over by the time he goes home on furlough." Such a statement is only a demonstration of the prevailing ignorance in this country about missionary work. Unless he is building on another's foundation, the missionary will never have a worker prepared to take full responsibility for the work in just one term. If he could, there would be no excuse for his going back to that place. But it just doesn't happen.

And of course when the independent missionary dies or has to leave the field permanently, he has even less choice. The best thing is to ask some mission to take over the work. But what happens more often is that the work is abandoned.

NONPROFESSIONAL MISSIONARIES

We have already said what the nonprofessional missionaries are. In one sense they are independent, for they are not definitely connected with a mission society. In another sense they are not, for they seldom attempt a complete missionary ministry apart from what others are doing. They might rather be called auxiliary missionaries.

There are some very real values in the service of these part-time missionaries. One value is the same as the value of the testimony of the Christian businessman in the United States. It helps people to realize that Christianity is not just for the preachers; it is a vital faith in everyday life. Rightly or wrongly, some people get the idea that Christianity for the preacher is a livelihood; for the businessman it is a conviction.

Besides this, the businessman can sometimes reach individuals and even groups that are closed to the missionary. In his contacts with other businessmen and in his relations with government officials he can often speak a word in season about his Saviour. He may even get into a lengthy discussion of the Christian faith. People don't think this is inappropriate in other lands, where religious discussions are often more common than in America.

A third advantage of the nonprofessional missionary is that he may at times get an entrance into lands that are closed to regular missionaries. That is, he gets in not as a missio~ but as a businessman, an engineer, a professor. ~

wise and tactful in his approach he may prove the opening wedge for the full proclamation of the Gospel at a later date. At any rate he can commend it by his sincere profession of faith and Christian manner of living.

But don't think that there are no handicaps! There are a number of them, and they ought to be clearly understood. If you understand them they will take away the false impression that this is an easier and more effective way of doing missionary work. It is surprising how many get that false idea. It is a valuable service, and one in which we wish there were many more Christians engaged. But it is not easy; and its effectiveness is not to be compared with that of the full-time missionaries. Here are three of the reasons.

First, the one who is hired to do any secular job is expected to give full-time service on that job. He is not paid to be a missionary but to be a geologist, an engineer, a doctor, or whatever his profession or vocation is. It is only his spare time that he can devote to missionary work. That is, aside from casual conversations in the course of his work. And after a full day of hard work, it takes real consecration to take on other responsibilities of a missionary sort. Of course, too, his Christian service is limited to the immediate neighborhood of the place where he works. He is not free to take any long trips except on vacation.

A second handicap is often found in the nature of his work. Most such men are in the employ of American companies. So naturally the people think of them primarily as employees of the company. Their interests are the same as the company's interests. If the people think, as they often do, that the company is exploiting them for its own advantage, then its foreign employees are a part of the plan. If they preach the Gospel, it is so the people will be more pliable tools of the company. Even full-time missionaries are accused of being paid agents of the American government. It is no wonder that an employee of a large American firm is suspected, and with much better reason.

Finally, the one who plans to be a nonprofessional missionary may find himself seriously hampered by the ones he works for and with. The company itself is not likely to be very much interested in his purpose. Not that it is opposed to Christianity as such. Rather, it just doesn't want its employees engaged in any activities that might put the company in a bad light and jeopardize its earnings. In some countries this may not be much of a problem. In others, as in strongly Muslim countries, it may be a serious one.

Then too, the worker needs to realize that he may be working in a non-Christian land with fellow Americans who are also non-Christian in their manner of living. That is, many of those who go overseas for business reasons may be members of Christian churches at home, but they appear to leave their Christian principles, with their membership, at home. As Dan Crawford once wrote about Central Africa, "In this climate European meat goes bad, European dogs go bad, and European morals go bad."

The worker may be fortunate enough to find some good Christian fellowship in his work. There are indeed a number of fine Christian businessmen to be found in many lands. But in most cases the situation will be just the opposite. He must be prepared to stand alone, if need be, and to resist the constant pull that would bring him down to the level of the others. His very loneliness will make the temptations all the stronger.

No, it is not an easy service, and the visible results are often disappointing. But it is a valuable service, *principally for those who could not qualify for full-time missionary service.*

This is one thing that must be borne in mind. It is for those who have not been called to a full-time ministry but are willing to carry on their trade or profession in a foreign land, where their witness for Christ may help bring men to Him. If supposedly Christian businessmen abroad were as zealous for their faith as are the Muslim traders in Africa, what a tremendous effect their witness could have!

CHAPTER XX

WHAT A MISSIONARY DOES

THE TITLE OF THIS CHAPTER is presumptuous—almost ridiculous. Who could possibly compress into a chapter or two all the multitude of activities in which missionaries engage? And who could describe the activities of a missionary in Latin America and presume that the same ones would be carried on in New Guinea?

Yet it seems wise to attempt some sort of description of a missionary's ministry. The major reason is that people at home have conjured up such a fictitious idea of a missionary's life that they need a corrective. And the young people who are volunteering for missionary service ought to have some idea of what that service is to be.

Actually, in spite of the great variety of missionary activities, there are some that are common to all lands and to most missionaries. There are also some principles that are valid everywhere, though the way we apply them will differ in different circumstances. And we are not going to try to give a complete picture. We are going to concentrate on just a few features, trusting that this rough sketch will be reasonably accurate and suggestive of the many details that we shall have to omit.

Judging from the questions they ask, most people seem to think of the missionary as a sort of combination itinerant evangelist and handyman. They usually think he has a rather hard life, though some would insist that the picture has been overdrawn and that missionaries really lead a sort of life of Riley among the poverty-stricken natives. They do agree that there must be something of glamour and adventure in his life. All faraway lands and strange people are glamorous from a distance.

As for the missionary's work, they think it consists almost entirely of preaching sermons and getting people to join his church. Of course they know his work involves travels and dangers—look at David Livingstone! And the missionary may have to turn builder or medicine man on occasion. But most of all he preaches to ignorant, uncultured natives.

Let's see if we can give something that will help to correct this distorted view. It is not enough to say that it is wrong. It is not enough to remind people that the world is changing and that we are not living in the days of Livingstone. We need to paint a truer picture of what a missionary is and does.

THE NEW MISSIONARY

The first task of the new missionary is to go to school. It might seem that after all his years of preparation in the homeland he would now be ready to begin his ministry. But it is not so. In most cases he still has to learn the language of the people to whom he is going to minister. And it is no small task.

In fact, because it is such a task, there are always some who try to short-cut language study. More than ever since World War II there have been many who have tried to carry on a ministry through interpreters. From some places, as Japan, they have sent home marvelous reports of the success of their efforts. When some have questioned whether the results were not more apparent than real, they have become indignant. One young student, a member of a youth team, vehemently insisted that they had wonderful results—he had seen them himself! How could he know what was going on in the minds of the people, when he couldn't understand a word they said?

Interpretation has its values. It is useful when the people are so interested in the speaker himself that they are anxious to get any sort of message from him. It isn't the message so much as the speaker who interests them. It is also useful when the speaker has a message whose importance they recognize and which they can't get in any other way. They know they won't get it perfectly, but at least they will get some of the main ideas.

Speaking by interpretation is always a poor substitute for speaking in the language of the people. I remember with amusement the introduction a Central American pastor gave me to his congregation, a congregation that had had to listen to a number of interpreted messages during the preceding months. In concluding his introduction he remarked, "You will be able to understand *him*. He speaks our language!"

To realize the ineffectiveness of the interpreted message, just put yourself in the place of the other person. Suppose a Buddhist missionary came to your community to try to win converts for his faith, but he could not speak English. Since he has come from an oriental country, you might be curious to see and hear him for a time or two. You would have to sit twice as long as usual to get his message, since he first says a few things in his own tongue and then the interpreter tries to tell what he means in English.

If the interpreter is too fluent in his interpretation, you wonder just how much of his own ideas he has put in. Or if the interpreter is a convinced Buddhist, and so can interpret with fluency, you wonder why he doesn't do the preaching himself. Except, of course, that a foreigner attracts the curious. And if the interpreter is obviously very careful to interpret accurately, and so rather awkwardly, what happens to the oratory, the fine reasoning, the warm passion of the speaker? These are things that can't be interpreted on the spur of the moment.

And of course if interpretation is not very effective in

evangelizing, it is much less so in teaching, in building up and guiding a newly founded church, etc. Yet these things are most important in sound missionary work. There is really no substitute for the accurate learning of the native language by the missionary. Short cuts are really blind alleys.

There are various ways in which new missionaries learn the language. The best way is usually the language school. Sometimes a large mission, like the China Inland Mission, conducts its own language school. At other times, as in India, the language school is a sort of joint enterprise, and missionaries from all missions attend. The language school has several advantages. It usually has a carefully planned course, experienced teachers who give full time to the job, and no other obligations to distract the new missionary from his main job of learning the language.

For French, Belgian and Portuguese territories in Africa, the missionaries have to learn at least two languages. They must know the language of the government as well as that of the tribe in which they work. This usually means language study in Europe for perhaps a year before going on to Africa.

In many other cases missionaries are taught on their stations by the senior missionaries or by nationals hired to do the teaching. Unless the national is adept in both languages it often works out best to have a missionary teach the grammar, while the national teaches pronunciation, conversation and reading.

Of course there are some languages that have not yet been reduced to writing and for which there are no grammars written. Here the missionary has real need for the special linguistic training available in the homeland. Also he must expect that it will take him much longer to learn the language than others who have the advantage of grammars, dictionaries, teachers, etc.

The length of time for language study varies. Some languages are more difficult for Americans than others. In the

Spanish language school at San José, Costa Rica, the normal period is one year of three fifteen-week terms. The students spend at least four hours a day in the classroom. At the close of the three terms, if the student has done satisfactorily, he is considered ready to enter the work. He is still far from having a complete mastery of the language, but he has a good working basis. His mission may require further study and reading on the field.

Sometimes people who never had to learn another language wonder why it takes so long. They think there must be some easier way. They point to the fact that little children seem to "pick up" a language in a short time and wonder why older people can't do the same.

There are several reasons. Little children often get a better pronunciation than their parents because their habits of pronunciation in English are not so fixed that it is hard for them to adjust to new sounds. Then, too, they are not so afraid of being embarrassed. They try to mimic the words and expressions they hear, repeat them over and over to themselves, and blurt them out at every opportunity, even when they don't fit. What if they do make a mistake? No one takes them seriously and it helps them to learn.

But aside from this little children are very limited in their conversation. If the missionary were willing to confine himself to childish prattle he wouldn't need to study so long. A proper use of the language, however, in presenting the profound truths of the Gospel calls for much more than this. After all, how many years do we have to study English in our schools to become acceptable ministers of God's Word? Even though we started to speak it before we were two years old.

What most Americans fail to realize is that learning another language is not just learning a new set of words to take the place of our English words. Language is a means of expressing thought. And the thoughts of other people are not always similar to our thoughts; neither do they use the same manner of expressing similar thoughts.

For instance, we have a common word "to lack." But Holman Bentley tells us that in a certain tribe in the Congo there is no one word that bears that meaning. If you mean "to lack something you never had," you use a different word from the one for "to lack what you once possessed." Americans studying Spanish are always confused by the fact that a Spanish-speaking person never "likes" anything; instead, the thing "is pleasing to him."

So the new missionary is faced with the problem not only of memorizing a complete new set of words, with an entirely different sort of pronunciation, but of learning new patterns of thinking and new ways of expressing thought. Through the language he begins his job of getting into the life of the people. He must understand them, and they must understand him, or else his ministry will be in vain.

We have dealt rather extensively with this first task of the new missionary. This is because it is so little understood or appreciated at home, and yet is so vital on the field. If we were to pick out one of the most glaring weaknesses in the missionary enterprise as a whole, it would certainly be the failure of so many missionaries to get a good command of the native tongue.

But the new missionary has another important job. It is to learn to know the people. At the same time that he is studying the language, he is learning something about the people. But he needs to know more. Sometimes a veteran of many years will say, "I suppose we never do get to think just the way the people do. Maybe that's why we're not more effective."

But whether the missionary ever does get to think just exactly as the people do, he tries to understand them as best he can. That is an important part of his ministry. He must try to follow Christ, the master missionary, in this, identifying himself as much as possible with the people to whom he is sent. If he doesn't entirely succeed, we still know that he has probably gotten closer to the heart of the people than any other outsiders.

It is no wonder that missionaries on furlough sometimes speak of the people as "my people" and "my tribe." It is perhaps less often that the people speak of the missionary as one of themselves. Yet one Presbyterian missionary in Shantung had the experience of being adopted as a daughter into a Chinese family. And in Japan a missionary won popular approval by attending classes in school with Japanese children so that she might learn their language better.

The missionary doesn't think of his learning to know the people as a job. It isn't a subject that he can very well study in the classroom. Yet it does take a good deal of time and attention.

He soon finds that you can only learn to know them as you come into personal contact with them. He must visit much with them in their homes. He must eat with them, perhaps dipping his fingers into the same bowl of food. He must enter into their sport, where it doesn't conflict with Christian principles. He must also enter into their sorrows—you can learn more about the people at a wake than at a church service. He must welcome them into his own home and perhaps spend long hours talking—about nothing in particular.

It all takes time, time that impatient Americans often think could be better spent at more productive tasks. But this is the very foundation of productiveness. You must win the confidence of the people if you want them to trust your message. And confidence is not something that can be won overnight, especially by a foreigner.

JUST LIVING

Often the missionary doesn't want to tell the folks at home about this, for fear they won't understand. In fact he sometimes finds it irritating to himself and wishes he could do more about it. But in spite of his desires he has to keep on spending a lot of time and energy with the details of just living.

What we mean is this. We scarcely realize in the homeland how convenient life has been made for us with a multitude of aids to living. It is not only with such ultramodern helps as electric dishwashers, garbage disposal units and air conditioning. It is rather the many conveniences that we take for granted.

Not many of our young people today know what it means to clean and trim a kerosene lamp. They flip a switch and have light. When they want a drink, they go to the faucet or the water cooler, with never a thought as to the purity of the water. They can buy all of their food in one store, most of it in cans or jars. If they do any baking or canning, it is through economy or preference, not need. We even buy our bread already sliced.

These are just some of the common things. In fact, the only thing that keeps other items from being more widely used than they are, such as vacuum cleaners, refrigerators, etc., is a lack of money. Even in remote areas they can all be had from the mail order house.

And what of the missionary? Sometimes he can have some of these helps, too. Where he can, so much the better, but often he can't. The only way to have electricity in many mission stations is to put in your own plant. This sounds easy, but have you ever tried to keep an electric light plant in regular operation for a long period of time, without a repairman nearer than a day's journey? Even if you're a competent mechanic yourself, it will take some of your time.

And drinking water. Boiling the water for drinking is just routine for many a missionary family. And sometimes it has to be both filtered and boiled. That takes time. Even the stove may be a problem. Of course gas stoves and electric stoves are out. Kerosene and gasoline stoves are often used, but they do need attention, with often a clogged generator to clean or replace, or a troublesome wick to attend to.

And then the food. How often the missionaries remember with longing the corner grocery in the homeland! Of course if there is a daily market the missionary can go there and see what is available. Though sometimes his wife will have to wait until he gets home to know what they will have for dinner. It saves time to hire someone else to do the marketing—but not money. And naturally, there are not many prepared foods!

In more and more mission fields the automobile is proving its usefulness as roads are being built. But again automobiles mean repairs, and repairs take time. But for all that, even in the old days, when most missionaries counted themselves fortunate to have a good horse or mule for traveling, it took a lot of time to feed and care for these animals.

What we have tried to do here is to give some impression of the many "chores" that occupy so much of a missionary's time. We have only touched the fringe, and of course we know that the situation is different in every field. But if you ask any missionary you will find that he has to spend a lot more time than he wants to, just on the details of living in a foreign land.

CHAPTER XXI

WHAT A MISSIONARY DOES
(*Continued*)

LEAVING ASIDE some of the other details that fill up a missionary's life—letters, reports, dealing with government officials, and the like—let's turn for a brief view of five major missionary activities: evangelism, counseling, church establishment, teaching and literature.

EVANGELISM

When we talk about evangelism, everyone thinks immediately of *preaching*. And of course the missionary does preach. He preaches whenever and wherever he can. It may be in a church building; it may be in the open air. It may be in a city street chapel, where people are continually coming and going; it may be in the village council house, where they have gathered especially to hear his message. It may be in a large convention, or in a neighborhood meeting held in somebody's hut.

He often preaches more than his minister in the homeland. I remember the amusement of a mission director as he told me about an applicant to his society. The young man apparently thought he would impress the mission with his abilities and experience. "I think I would be able to do the work all right," he wrote. "I'm used to preaching. I preach at least twice every Sunday and once in the middle of the week, be-

sides occasional sermons at other times." The director laughed
and said, "I told him we didn't have a missionary on our field
who preached that little!"

Oh, it isn't always the best of preaching in a homiletic sense.
It may have to be much less formal. How can you develop a
theme with a firstly, secondly, and thirdly when you are
preaching in a market where most of the people just stop for
a few minutes and then move on? It is like street corner
preaching in the homeland.

And many times you can't get by with a ten or fifteen min-
ute sermonette. The people are there to hear God's message
and it may be a long time before they will get another chance.
They want "the whole counsel of God"—or at least as much
of it as they can get. Some of them came many miles on foot
just to hear that message. So keep on, preacher; give them
good measure!

Late one Saturday a dusty traveler reached our home. He
was a Christian from a town where there were no other believers. He had trudged two or three days on foot to reach our
city. He stayed with us over Sunday, and early Monday morning he started back, another two or three days' journey. "Every
once in awhile," he told us, "I get so hungry for Christian fellowship that I just have to come down here for a Sunday and
hear a sermon or two. Now I'm going back well fed."

The invitation is a standard part of an evangelistic meeting in the United States. At the close of the sermon, sometimes
while the congregation sings a hymn, people are urged to accept Christ and to indicate their decision by raising their
hand.

In many mission fields this just doesn't work. As a missionary to Africa wrote, "If we did such a thing, every hand in the
place would go up! But it wouldn't mean anything." "If
people are really converted," say others, "they ought to be
able to stand up and say so."

And they do. On a recent visit to Puerto la Cruz, Venezuela, my sermon was interrupted right in the middle by a woman who stood and said, "I want to accept Christ as my only and sufficient Saviour!" Then she sat down. Nobody was shocked, nobody thought it was unusual, and after a pause the sermon went on.

Of course *personal evangelism* is the foundation of all evangelistic work. After the beginning, the people themselves do most of it. But the real missionary never ceases to be a personal evangelist and some give a great deal of time to it. Even in many of his talks with groups, the missionary often just "gossips the Gospel."

Some missionaries spend a good deal of time *traveling*. They have to if they are to do a good job. You see, the missionary is not supposed to be a settled pastor, ministering to one congregation. His work is broader than that.

Now travel always sounds attractive to those who like to read books of travels. Sometimes they get just enough of a taste of it during a summer vacation to wish they could do more. But that is in this country, where everybody travels and traveling is made easy.

It's not always so on the mission field. There have been many improvements in travel in recent years. The word safari in much of Africa no longer means a long line of porters trudging single file down a trail bearing the missionary's equipment, and sometimes the missionary himself. Now the missionary may pile everything into a station wagon or truck and take along just a helper or two when he travels. In some places, even in primitive areas like the jungles of eastern Ecuador, he has the airplane at his call. But that doesn't mean that travel is easy. Or that it no longer takes much time.

Take the missionary in India, for example. Suppose he wants to go on a tour of the villages of his district. There are airplanes in India, but they wouldn't do him much good for such local travel. There are railroads in India, even if they may not be up to our American standards. But the railroads aren't much help in reaching many of these villages. So the missionary takes a truck, and as far as he can makes use of the highways.

He will have to plan his trip carefully and take a great deal more equipment than we might imagine necessary. In the first place he's not likely to find a hotel or a rooming house where he can stay; so he takes a tent. That means, too, all the equipment for sleeping, washing and eating. For of course he can't just drop in at a restaurant, come mealtime. And even if there is a market where foods are prepared in the open air, he finds it wiser to get his meals cooked under his own supervision.

Then there are the implements of his work. He may have to have a portable organ along, or some other musical instrument. There are tracts, Scriptures and other books for those who read. Charts, flannelgraphs and other such aids help reach both the children and the older people. It may be that he can even take along a projector and show slides, using his truck to provide the electricity.

But the missionary to India has an easy time traveling compared to some of the missionaries among the lowland Indians of South America. Sometimes these missionaries have the advantage of airplane transportation to and from their stations. That is a tremendous help. But it does involve work that we do not always remember. An airplane must have a place to land—a large, level, cleared space, free of trees, stumps and underbrush. It is a real job to make such a clearing, even with plenty of cheap labor available. It is also a job to keep it clear, for in the moist tropics vegetation seems to spring up overnight.

Then, too, the missionary must have some way of contacting the plane when he needs it. That means short-wave radio communication. Which is all very lovely until the set gets out of order. And of course no one can tell when or how often that may happen.

However, the plane is not used for the ordinary tours the missionary makes. It is useful only for the big hops. On the ground sometimes trucks can be used—yes, even where the government has spent little or no money on road building. One group of missionaries in Bolivia built their own road so that trucks could get to their station. Of course it was a rough job, and in such places the truck needs a power winch to pull itself out of mud holes. But it was usable, just as in some other places dry stream beds are usable as roads during the dry season.

But beyond the roadhead there is still need for traveling. There is much less travel by foot today than there once was, but the inland waterways are still an extremely important highway system. Whether it be by motor boat or canoe, the traveler in the interior sooner or later has to take to the "flowing road."

We Americans are losing the fine art of *visitation*. That is, the pleasant and sometimes stimulating conversations which once were the very heart of a visit are rapidly losing out. Now, when visitors appear, they must put up with a third party who tends to monopolize the conversation, a party to whom nobody can answer back—the radio. Or they face the even more formidable competition of the TV set, which demands the attention of both eyes and ears. It likewise gives you no chance to discuss the question—if indeed it is worth discussing.

Even pastoral visitation is becoming a rarity. Pastors are too busy with a score of other activities that seem more important. (Or is their "busy-ness" just a cover-up for an aversion to a task that is so spiritually demanding?) In some cases a "church visitor" is employed, usually a woman, who has a hard time convincing anybody that her visit is much of a substitute for the pastor's. But in most cases the visiting just isn't done.

Visitation on most mission fields, however, still holds much of its former position of importance. The visitor is usually welcomed. He is welcomed even when his host disagrees radically with his point of view. After all, how are you going to understand the other's point of view if you don't talk with him? And if you want an opening for personal evangelism, here it is.

Some years ago I made a sort of survey trip out along the Gulf of Paria in Venezuela. In the small port of Cristobal Colon I was held up for about a week, waiting for a way to proceed homeward. While there I spent considerable time visiting among the people, without positive results so far as I could see.

Two or three years later, after our return from furlough, the missionary then in charge of that district was visiting in our home. "You will be interested," he said, "in a report I just got from up the coast. Do you remember a woman in Cristobal Colon who was very much interested in the Gospel when you were out that way?"

I told him I couldn't remember any such person. But then I had done a good deal of visiting in the town.

"Well, anyway," he continued, "this woman says you spent a lot of time one day explaining the Gospel to her and several others. She wasn't quite ready to accept it then; but she did later. And now word has come saying that she has died trusting in the Saviour, thanks to your visit."

And still, the most that I ever could remember was that one day a storekeeper had courteously offered me a chair outside his little store. His wife and a number of others had gathered around, as in a leisurely fashion we carried on our conversation. An hour? Two hours? I really don't know how long we talked. But that woman may have been one of the group.

COUNSELING

Visiting is often closely associated with the work of counseling. Whether in the homeland or on the mission field, those who need our counsel do not always seek us out. Many a time we must go and find them.

Now counseling is a most demanding sort of work. Young people who have never occupied places of leadership don't understand just how demanding it can be. They are likely to think of it simply as the giving of advice.

The proverb about the cheapness of advice probably started because there is so much cheap advice in circulation—cheap, not only because it is given without charge but because it didn't even cost the giver so much as a few minutes of serious thought.

Opinions and superficial advice are easy to express. But what if a life depended on your judgment? What if following your advice might possibly bring anguish and remorse? And if it meant the eternal destiny of a soul?

Every missionary is called upon for counsel. Not for just the common spiritual problems which confront the pastor or the Christian worker here in the homeland. The variety of subjects on which the counsel of the missionary is sought is astounding. Somehow he is expected to be an authority on almost every subject under the sun. Yet he knows that he is not.

What is he going to do? To some of the people he has become a spiritual father. And fatherhood means care. Are the children to be blamed if they don't understand just what kind of subjects their father can best counsel them about? Isn't he supposed to know? How can they tell the difference between a spiritual problem, a social problem, and an economic problem? Just what is the difference?

Counseling takes a lot of time. Perhaps there is no other job the missionary has that is more time-consuming. Even when a man comes to you for counsel, he may beat around the bush for a long time before he comes to the point. And even then it may take a bit of prying to find out what really is the heart of the matter. Ask any dean of students.

And no job calls for more understanding. This is one of the

reasons why missions want young people who are mature in thinking and acting. Maturity of experience shows itself more in counseling than perhaps anywhere else. In counseling as in medicine the first problem is to diagnose the case. It calls for patience to lead the person to reveal just what is the trouble—patience and obvious sympathy that will inspire confidence. It takes discernment to see just what is the issue involved, and then to restate the case in such a way that the person himself will see it. It takes tact and self-control to avoid saying, "This is what you'll have to do," and to say instead, "This is what your decision will mean; but the decision is up to you."

It is in this field of counseling that the missionary can show his spiritual leadership. It is important from the beginning and it continues to grow in importance. There will come a time when native evangelists and pastors will do the preaching, when native teachers will displace the missionary teacher and even take over the work of the supervisor. But there will still be a need for the counselor, for the one to whom they can turn in confidence to help them solve the many problems they face.

THE CHURCH

We have already said that a part of the aim of missions is to establish the church. This should be the natural result of evangelism. In fact a working fellowship of believers must result if the evangelism is to have any permanent effect. So one of the missionary's most vital tasks is to help the church get started and guide it in its early years. It also takes plenty of tact and spiritual leadership.

The faith missions, which have always strongly emphasized evangelism, gave comparatively little attention to the church until recent years. Their emphasis on evangelism was needed. But they found that after the first advances the work did not progress as it should. Instead of becoming every year stronger and more vigorous, it showed signs of weakness. It continued to depend too much on the presence of the foreign missionary. They came to realize, at least in part, that without reducing their zeal for evangelism they needed to place more emphasis on the building up of the church.

Looking back now, it is easy to say that we should have known better. Didn't Paul lay great emphasis on the church in all his missionary work? Wasn't that part of the secret of his success? But we should realize that there are still many, both in the faith missions and in the denominational missions, who have not yet learned that lesson. They are not convinced that the principles used in the first century can be applied today. The circumstances are different.

But on the whole, missions are laying greater stress on the church today than before. Especially since World War II and the closing of China we have seen the importance of developing a strong national church which is not dependent on the missionaries. And to this matter the missionary has to give a great deal of attention.

We are used to churches in the United States. Even though our churches differ somewhat in their organization and procedures, there is a great deal of similarity between them. Fundamentally, they are all voluntary associations in which the members have a great deal to say about what is done. Whether the pastor is appointed by a bishop or chosen by vote of the congregation, his authority is limited by the will of the people. Democratic procedures are the rule, procedures with which we become acquainted as early as our grade school days. And there is so much similarity in the usual order of service that a visitor might find it difficult to tell the denomination of the church he is in, unless he already knows it. Most of us are familiar with these things from childhood.

This is not true in many mission fields. The people's manner of life has been entirely different. Society is organized on a different basis from what it is in the United States. Many haven't the foggiest notion of what democracy is, or what democratic procedures would be. A large part of them are used to chiefs, to dictators of one sort or another. And they think it only natural that these things should be carried into their church life.

For example, a young Bible school graduate in a South American country went to be the pastor of a church. His country was one of those which have usually been run by strong-armed dictators. He had been taught parliamentary rules and church government in his Bible school days. But it is hard for a few years of formal teaching to overrule a lifetime of experience.

Within a short time he got into trouble with his church officers and some of the older members over, of all things, their political views. Without bothering to follow parliamentary procedure, he promptly excommunicated all of those who disagreed with him. "Long live the dictator!" Fortunately he didn't last long.

Church life is something entirely new to many people. Their religious life has been on an entirely different basis. Religion is more a part of daily life than it is here, but regular weekly services may be lacking. And of course witch-doctors don't preach sermons. Besides, religion is often a community affair—the whole town or tribe has a single religion, with no dissenters allowed. So it is quite a new thing to come into a church—an *ekklesia,* or "called-out group." How does one act in a church, and how does the church act in society?

We can't go into the details of this problem. But we trust we have said enough to show that it is something to which the missionary has to give long, careful and prayerful attention. How to lead the people to understand the Scriptural ideal of the church? How much of our American church organization to introduce? (We Americans love to organize to the limit— or even beyond it!) How much of the native pattern of life to adapt to church purposes? When to stay in the background and allow them to run things—letting them make their own mistakes instead of making them all ourselves? How to encourage the development of a native leadership? And so on, without end.

One thing is certain: the church will usually take on a much greater importance in the life of the people than it has at present in our American life. We have turned over so much to the state and to secular organizations—education, charity, relief, social affairs—that the church does little more than minister to what we call the "strictly spiritual." Even in a funeral service the mortician rather than the minister is in charge of affairs.

But in mission lands the situation is different. In fact, because it is so different many of our American missionaries find it difficult to understand and to adjust their planning and acting. You see, in coming into the church the people have had to come out of non-Christian society, have had to break many of their former connections. It is not just a matter of attending a different type of religious service. They have to build a different life.

Sometimes they may have to find a different way of earning a living. A maker of idols cannot continue in that craft. He may need help to get something else. Usually their social life is changed. Sometimes the change is only in the companions; the activity itself is good—as in some games. At other times an activity is completely dropped—as with drinking parties, gambling and lewd dances. Then something else must be put in its place, for man is a social being.

It is in the church that people have found spiritual life. In the church they find a new and delightful fellowship. So it is only natural that they look to the church in any other case of need.

Just before the recent war in Korea, the Yung Nak Presbyterian Church started in Seoul. It was a refugee church, one among many. The pastor had managed to escape from the terror in North Korea, and in the capital he found many other North Korean refugees. They met for worship and soon there was no auditorium large enough for the multitude of refugee Christians.

But they did other things. They all knew what it was to abandon all their possessions and escape to a strange part of the country where they had no home, no job, no friends but their fellow Christians. So through the church those who arrived first began to help later arrivals. As they were able, they provided them with food. For some they supplied clothing. They set up a sort of employment bureau and helped many to get jobs. Then as each one got on his own feet he began to take a part in helping others.

They didn't question whether this was the church's job. From where else should help come if not from their brethren in Christ?

CHAPTER XXII

WHAT A MISSIONARY DOES
(*Concluded*)

LEADERSHIP TRAINING

YOU CAN'T HAVE CHURCHES without leaders. The leaders may not be given titles, but they are leaders just the same. The question is, what type of leaders are you going to have, and how well will they be prepared for their task?

Of course it is entirely possible for the missionary himself to take the place of leadership. In some ways that is easiest, for you have no training problems and no question about whether the work will continue in the way you have it planned. But the poor missionary soon finds himself burdened down with responsibilities without number. And in spite of all his efforts the church doesn't seem to progress. If he were to have to leave the field, as has happened, the work would fall to pieces.

Another alternative is to note those who seem to have the gift of leadership and turn over to them at least a part of the responsibilities. It might work. That is, it might work if the one appointed has more than the usual amount of humility, tact, patience, perception of spiritual principles, and a few other gifts. But the odds are against it. Paul knew what he was talking about when he wrote against giving leadership to a "neophyte," a novice. He knew the danger of pride, the danger that such a man would fall into the enemy's trap. It has happened time and again. More than natural ability is needed in the leadership of the church.

The only satisfactory plan is to train leaders. But that is not as simple as it sounds. You can't just pick out a promising young man, send him away to school for a few years, and have him come back all ready to do the leading.

In the first place, the missionary's choice of leaders is not always the best choice. Many a time the missionary has selected and sponsored the schooling of a young man, only to find that he is not accepted as a leader by his people. Sometimes the very fact that the missionary has chosen him is a handicap. He is the missionary's stooge, not a leader raised up from among the people. He may feel the resentment that we all express toward a teacher's pet.

It is not always easy to find the Lord's choice for leadership. He may be, like David, the one considered least likely. As Samuel said, "Man looketh on the outward appearance; but God looketh on the heart." So the missionary has to be careful not to rush ahead and anoint the first promising candidate. He may have to try them out for a long time first. Then he may be able to commend some to the church as Paul commended Timothy when he sent him to Philippi: "I have no man like-minded, who will naturally care for your state. For all seek their own, not the things which are Jesus Christ's. But ye know the proof of him . . ."

Second, training for leadership isn't just a matter of sending young people away to school for a few years. In fact, there are not many schools that are good training grounds for leadership. Sometimes the best students are those who conform most readily to the pattern, who faithfully and intelligently do what they are told, but lack the initiative, the imagination, the aggressiveness that a leader must have. The leader may sometimes be a headache to the dean. He goes off into paths that the teacher hadn't thought of, and raises questions that are not covered by his set lectures.

The first place for leadership training is right at home, in the home congregation. And that means more work for the missionary. It is up to him to encourage these young people to do things. And then to counsel them in the doing. It is up to him to introduce them to the treasures of the Scriptures and show how they can be used in daily living. It is up to him to put before them the challenge of loving service for Christ. It is up to him to bear them on his heart in prayer that the Lord will help them out into an effective witness for Him.

You can't have *Christian* leadership without Bible study. But Bible study must be given to more than the leaders. The wise missionary realizes this and plans regular Bible teaching for all the people. The Bible teaching in the Korean churches has been a model in this regard. What good is it to have the leaders instructed if the people are kept in ignorance? It will not be long before the leaders too are dragged down. The whole level of the church must be raised. And this is a blessed task, but a big one.

But neither can you have leadership unless the leader is ahead of the people. This means special training. It was strongly impressed on me when a woman from the Women's Bible Class in a certain station came to me one day. She said, "Mr. Cook, we love our teacher. We admire her Christian life and her sweet spirit. But can't you do something to help her? She doesn't know any more than we do!" It is one of the problems of missionary life that those who are the most willing to be of service are not always the most able. And those who are the most able in other ways lack the devotion, the self-sacrificing zeal of the less capable.

How can you inspire a gifted young person to give his life in the Lord's service when the world offers so many more material advantages? How can the missionaries in Africa turn their talented young pupils to the ministry, when they see the pastors living in need, and the government offers them a comfortable living? How can you take the humble young people of one talent—but with lots of devotion—and help them to polish that one talent and use it with such effect that they can be called true leaders of the church of Christ? How? The missionary would like to know. In his work he needs to know. That's part of his job.

Just a word about our Bible schools. We have them in nearly every field. They're doing a most important job. But they've got a lot of problems the folks at home don't know about. It sounds thrilling at home to talk about training native preachers. Just think how much better they will be able to do the job than the missionary! How much more the missionary's work will count if he gives his time to this teaching ministry!

As a matter of fact these statements are largely true. The trouble is that not every missionary is qualified for the job. And in reality it is one of the hardest of all jobs to do well. Besides, it isn't as romantic as it may sound.

It isn't a job for the newcomer. Sometimes a young missionary candidate in the homeland tells the mission board that he has been called to teach in the Bible school. He has never had any experience in that sort of work but he thinks it would be interesting.

The director of a Bible institute told me of one such young man. He reached the field, studied the language, and then was actually assigned to the Bible institute. He spent just about a year there. Then he went to the director and said, "I was mistaken. I don't think this is the work for me. I'd like to be assigned to regular station work." And he was.

It is not just the fact that some people are teachers and others are not. Nor is it the fact that you really need to be familiar with the language before you can do a good job of teaching. This job calls for experienced workers because they are the ones who have come to know the people, know something of their background and something of what can be expected of them. Through their work in the field they know something of the situation that the graduates will face and they can plan their courses accordingly. You see, a good teacher has to know a lot more than just the subject he is to teach.

And then there are problems that we don't usually worry much about here in the United States. For instance, many of those who go to the Bible schools have had very little previous education. How can you expect study from people who have never learned to study? An hour or two of preparation for each class? Some of them have never studied an hour consecutively in their lives. That may mean more time in class and less time for study.

And how can you teach effectively without textbooks? By the lecture system? Our American students flounder badly enough under such a system. And those who have difficulty writing at all are at a complete loss in a lecture class. Yet textbooks are scarce in a large part of our fields. They are scarce because there has been no one to prepare them in the language of the people, or because there wouldn't be a large enough circulation to warrant the cost of printing them, or because there just isn't money available for the purpose.

And if you have a Bible school without many churches, what will happen to your graduates? Will they be willing to take several years for Bible training, and then go back to their old homes, to take up their former jobs and give voluntary part-time service to the church? Are there churches enough, and are they financially able to support all those who graduate? Will the young people feel that since you have trained them for Christian service you are responsible to see that they find suitable employment in Christian service? These problems are not imaginary; they are actually facing the missionaries on more than one field.

CHRISTIAN LITERATURE

We have spoken about the lack of textbooks for our Bible training schools, a situation that adds to the missionary's work. This is only one phase of our need for Christian literature in the mission fields today. Actually, *the two greatest challenges for missionary service today are in the field of leadership training and in that of Christian literature.* We are all aware of these needs, but we haven't met them yet. One of the major reasons is that, just as in leadership training, the requirements for doing a good job are very high.

Literature is not a job for the newcomer, no matter how well trained he may have been in the United States. There is much that he has to learn first. But if he has any talent at all, he can be practicing while he is learning and getting thoroughly equipped for this most important ministry.

First of all, of course, he has to learn the language. But he needs to know it much more thoroughly than the missionary who will use only the spoken language. When you are speaking you can use facial expressions and gestures to help put across your meaning. You can watch the people, and if they don't seem to be getting what you are saying you can say it in another way, until their faces brighten up with comprehension. You can even at times get your word order wrong and still be understood by emphasizing the proper places. But not so in writing. Every bit of the meaning including the emphasis must be carried by those black letters on white paper.

Then he has to get to know the people. This is for several reasons. He needs to know what should be written for them —what will prove of real value. But even more he needs to know just how to say it. Blunt, "straight-from-the-shoulder" writing such as we often use in English may not be acceptable to other people. And when it comes to illustrations, a high proportion of those that we use at home would never be understood in other places. Like the missionary who started to use the example of a railroad engineer in his sermon, and then suddenly realized that no one in his audience had ever seen a railroad train. The missionary needs to know the life of the people so as to write in terms that will be meaningful to them.

All of this means that the missionary must have experience on the field before he is ready for a ministry of writing. But he still needs something more. Not every experienced missionary can write. So he needs to have some talent for writing, an urge to do so, plus some instruction, together with plenty of practice. It doesn't matter too much that his writing instruction may have been in English. If he has learned to write clearly and forcefully in English he will learn to do a good job in the other language.

Those who engage in a literary ministry need to have a real devotion to their task. It is not very stimulating to sit down to a typewriter to put your thoughts on paper. It is much more inspiring to speak them to a living and responsive audience. Yet the audience of the writer is many times that of the speaker. And the words that he writes can be read and reread until they are all assimilated; whereas the speaker knows that his words are extremely perishable and must be grasped at the moment they are spoken, if ever.

We have been speaking of original writing. To some the answer to our need for Christian literature would seem to be the translation of what we already have in English. "We have so much good material in English," they say, "why can't you just translate it into the other language and be saved all that work of writing something original?" Missionaries often get this idea, too, and one of the first literary tasks a new missionary attempts is a bit of translation. It seems so easy.

But translation is far from easy. It is a hard job to make a smooth translation into another language which will be reasonably true to the sense of the original. You see, another language is not just another set of words, as we have said before.

It is another set of ideas, some of which are like ours, some are partly like ours, and others are quite different. The one who tries to translate word for word is sure to make ridiculous mistakes. One missionary tried to translate into Spanish the expression "spring of truth." He looked in the dictionary and found that the word *resorte* meant "spring," and used it. What he didn't know was that *resorte* is a spring like an automobile spring.

What makes translation particularly hard is that it always involves interpretation. You can't translate without interpreting. That is, you can't translate without having in your own mind a pretty clear idea of what the author was trying to say; because you are going to have to try to convey that same idea to an audience with a different background and through words and phrases quite different from those the author used.

Holman Bentley, in translating the Bible into a language of the Congo, found that there was no word for "brothers" in the general sense. There were separate words for brothers on the father's side, brothers on the mother's side, or full brothers born of both parents. In the passages which speak of the brothers of Christ he was faced with a problem. They could not be full brothers, since that would make Joseph Christ's father. He had two choices. He could call them brothers on the mother's side, which would mean that they were later children of Mary and Joseph. Or he could call them brothers on the father's side, which would make them children of Joseph by a previous marriage. Rightly or wrongly, he chose the latter. He had to interpret to translate.

Albert Schweitzer, who knew both German and French from childhood, refused to translate one of his books from one language to the other. He contended that the languages were so different it couldn't be done properly—even by the author himself. So he rewrote the whole work in French.

The literature problem is different on every field. Some missionaries go to fields where the language has not yet been reduced to writing. There the missionary has to begin from scratch. First he must patiently try to dig the spoken language out of the people, carefully recording all that he learns. He uses some system of phonetics in transcribing the sounds of the words he hears. After he has gathered a certain amount of information he uses those data to try to work out an alphabet for the language—a letter for each meaningful sound, and not more than one letter per sound.

As soon as he can understand a little, he tries to figure out the patterns of speech the people use—the grammar and syntax. Then when he can, he begins to try writing a few little things in their language. Of course they can't read them, but he reads them aloud to see if they are comprehensible. All of this takes time—a tremendous amount of time. Even with the improved methods of linguistic study it calls for years of devoted, patient application.

Writing the language is only the beginning. If it is to be useful the people must learn how to read it. So the missionary embarks on a literacy campaign, teaching the people to read and write their own language. Then they will be able to read for themselves the Word of God which he is trying to translate for them.

Literacy campaigns are not just for those who don't yet have a written language. Illiteracy faces the missionary in many fields that not only have written languages but a great deal of literature in those languages. The missionary rightly feels it is disgraceful when the people have the Bible in their own tongue but most of the Christians themselves are not able to read it. How can a church grow in such circumstances?

But literacy is only the opening of the door. Those who have learned to read can pass through. To what? What are they going to read? Obviously the most important single book is the Bible. But the whole Bible is such a task that it is seldom accomplished by a single missionary. Of the more than a thousand tongues into which some part of the Bible has been translated, the great majority still do not have the whole Bible.

We don't wait for the whole Bible, to provide other reading matter. Almost from the beginning the people will need hymns, for Christianity is a singing religion. Very few missionaries are poets and musicians, so they have to reverse the usual hymn-writing technique. They take an English or American hymn tune and then set words to it. The result may not be poetry, but it usually carries a message and is singable.

Another publication that is soon started, even among those who are just beginning to be literate, is the periodical. It may be just a four-page leaflet, or it may become a 16-page paper with illustrations. But it is issued at regular intervals and is much more important in the work than a similar paper would be here at home. But periodical publications call for a steady flow of writing, and they usually have to be printed on the field. The task is a big one.

Tracts are far more often read on the mission fields than they are at home. Sunday school literature is often scarce and so is greatly prized. Correspondence courses have proved their value wherever there is any sort of postal service, however poor. And always there is a call for Christian books: for Bible study books, devotional books, books on Christian doctrines, the home and family, on Christian history and biography, books for children, reference books. No one who has seen the pitifully small library of the non-English-speaking pastor in a foreign field can fail to be impressed by this ever-present need for more books.

The writing and printing of literature for the people is important. But equally important is the distribution of what is already available. The Bible colporteur is a familiar figure in the mission field. In many, notably in Latin America, he has been the pioneer to open the way for a more settled ministry. We can hardly overstress the importance of his work of seed-sowing. Colportage is one of the best ways of distributing not only the Bible but other Christian literature as well.

But there are also other ways. A full-time Gospel book-store is usually too big a job for the ordinary missionary to attempt, unless he is set apart for that ministry by the mission. But there are multitudes of missionaries who on their own initiative carry small stocks of books to sell to the people as they have opportunity. It is just one of the many odd jobs, and one whose profits are usually more spiritual than material.

Many a missionary, too, has his own private circulating library. To those who can't afford to buy a book he will lend one for a short time. Of course there is so much work in trying to keep track of the books that the library is in constant need of replenishing. But again it is time and money well spent. Books are meant to be read. And if good books are read there is bound to be some result.

Conclusion

What does a missionary do? He may not do everything that we have mentioned here. He most probably does a lot of other things that we haven't mentioned. There is no typical missionary, and there is no typical missionary work. Mission-aries have become "all things to all men, that they might by all means save some." What they do depends on the field and the circumstances where they are placed, on their own abilities and resources, and on the Lord's leading.

This we can say. There are some parts of a missionary's work which appeal to the people at home. These he learns to tell about in his missionary talks. But there may be other parts which are hard to make sound appealing. They may sound just like what they are—plain, tiring, even monotonous work. The second is just as much a part of the missionary's life as the first. Even more so. It probably consumes more of his time and more of his energies. And in many cases it is what really produces the results.

CHAPTER XXIII

A CHURCH MISSIONARY PROGRAM

W E HAVE ALREADY SAID something about the church's responsibility to missions. Now we want to come to some practical suggestions for carrying out that responsibility. It is the local church that we have in view, not the denomination. In fact, we want to think primarily of the church of average size, away from the major cities. These are the ones who would most appreciate help. They are also the ones from whom a great part of the help for missions must come.

The life of any missionary program in a local church depends largely on the leadership. Someone has to have the interest, the vision, the initiative and persistence to carry the program through. Normally the pastor should be that leader. People usually look to him for leadership, and in this matter they expect him to be better informed than the members. Besides, he must co-operate if missions is to be a church concern and not just a fringe activity of a small group in the church.

Now this doesn't always happen. The pastor isn't always willing or capable of taking the lead. Then it is up to someone else in the congregation, though he will have a much harder time. In any case it is important to win the support of the pastor. For purposes of our discussion here, we are going to assume that the pastor is the leader.

It is important that the pastor be sold on missions. That is, he needs to be really enthusiastic on the subject. The enthusiasms of the pastor tend to spread to the people. Not to everyone, but to many. And if the pastor is thoroughly convinced, the program is bound to follow. We may make suggestions that are helpful, but they are of no value apart from the hearty endorsement of the pastor. If he is only mildly interested, you may be sure that the program—even the most excellent program—will languish.

Three things the pastor needs to see if he is to be enthusiastic about missions. One is a matter that we have already treated, that the Scriptures present missions as essential in the church, and not as just an extra. Another is that the church itself will get a great blessing from taking a part in the work. This has been so amply proved by the experience of so many churches that sometimes we fear that a few pastors are taking up missions through wrong motives. They use them for their publicity value. A third thing, which is not always so readily recognized by the pastor of a small church, is that he and his church have a really important part to play in the work. In fact, a great many of our best missionary candidates come from small churches. And proportionately, some of the small churches are far more generous in their giving than the large ones.

When the pastor is really in earnest about a complete missionary program for his church, he will want to have before him several objectives. They may be stated as follows:

(1) To create interest and enthusiasm for missions on the part of as many members as possible. He may not be able to interest everybody, but he should try it. The more who are interested, the greater the blessing.

(2) To support that interest and enthusiasm with accurate and up-to-date information. Information is the food that interest grows on. But misinformation or out-of-date information can soon dull the appetite. It can't often be as up-to-date as the daily paper, and in some countries things don't change

very rapidly, but when you quote as present facts statements published more than thirty years ago (as I have heard on several occasions) you are on shaky ground.

(3) To secure as much prayer support for missions as possible. The missionaries on the field need this more than we realize. Their success depends on God's working through them rather than on their own unaided efforts.

(4) To contribute material support for missions in as large a measure as possible. This is one of the objectives, but don't think of it as the only one, nor even as necessarily the chief one.

(5) To provide personnel for the missionary enterprise. That is, to provide missionaries. It is surprising how many people are willing to give their dollars but not their sons and daughters.

(6) To train prospective missionaries as far as the local church can do that job. Sounds strange, doesn't it? How can a local church train a missionary? Well, just look back at the indispensables in missionary preparation and see how much can be done at home and through the home church.

(7) To assist in such other ways as its particular circumstances may enable it, such as the promotion of joint missionary conferences, etc. The church's objectives don't have to be limited to its own membership. Neither do its objectives have to be limited to the six mentioned above. Sometimes it can do more. And if it can, it should.

Now don't think that these objectives are separate and distinct from the other objectives of the church. They are closely related to them and sometimes actually blended with them. For instance, you can't busy yourself in the training of young people who may become missionaries without training some who will never be missionaries but will be better Christians. Actually you can hardly promote the missionary objectives of the church without benefiting the whole work of the church. The task abroad and the task at home are just two different

phases of the same task. The church exists for just two purposes: communion and evangelism. And evangelism in its
full sense embraces the whole world.

Now for some practical suggestions in connection with these
missionary objectives.

I. To create interest and enthusiasm for missions

  1. The pastor's own ministry

    Many a young pastor is called to a church which has
    little or no interest in missions. When he himself is
    vitally interested, he often asks, "How can I get my peo-
    ple interested, when they can't see it?"

    a. Don't try to force it on them. There is no surer way
      of turning disinterest into opposition. Missions must
      come from the heart. Your first job is to find out just
      where the people stand. Then beginning at that
      point try to lead them out step by step. If they al-
      ready have some sort of a missionary program, don't
      try to throw it out. Use it as a starting point for some-
      thing better.

    b. Get down to the fundamentals. Foreign missions is
      not the real issue. The real issue is a vitality of faith
      that constrains us to witness for Christ. When the
      church begins to feel its obligation to witness to
      others, missions will soon follow.

    c. Use missionary illustrations in your sermons. The
      story of missions is full of apt illustrations for most
      of the truths you will present in your regular preach-
      ing. You don't have to drag them in; they just fit. If
      your subject is persistence, you can find it illustrated
      in the life of William Carey, who claimed that as his
      only talent. If you are preaching on faith, Hudson
      Taylor can give you an excellent example. And it
      will be surprising if the people don't want to know
      more about these men after they have had a taste or
      two.

d. When the occasion offers, preach on missions. This is one of the advantages of expository preaching. It would be hard to give a series of messages on any extended passage in the New Testament without dealing with missions in normal course. You don't have to look for a reason to deal with it; it comes in naturally. Or if you follow the church calendar, Pentecost Sunday gives you an excellent occasion to speak on Missions—or Christmas Sunday.

2. Missionary speakers

Without doubt good missionary speakers can do more to stir up missionary interest than almost anyone else. But many pastors and leaders don't know how to get them or how to use them effectively.

a. Whom to invite

(1) Missionaries on furlough. These are usually the most popular speakers, because they can speak of their own experiences in the work. Many churches try to get missionaries "fresh from the field." Sometimes this may be all right, but many times the missionary needs to get a rest and get readjusted to home conditions and to a free use of the English language before he does much speaking. He will then do a better job.

(a) Those recommended by your denomination It is easy to get in touch with the deputational representative of your denomination's mission board and find out what missionaries may be available in your area, and when. But don't fail to ask for his recommendations. Some missionaries do best in a small gathering. Some have a special attraction for young people. Some, who are not gifted speakers, may be used only for a brief testimony.

(b) Those from well-known interdenominational missions

Independent churches as well as many denominational churches enjoy the inspiration brought by some of these missionaries. Unless you have a particular missionary in view and know that he is making his own appointments, just write to mission headquarters for information. Write a good deal ahead of time if possible. And again, don't hesitate to ask about the capabilities of those who may be available. Not every good missionary is a good public speaker.

(c) Others whom you may know or who may be recommended to you. Go slowly here. You are safest in inviting those who are from well-known missions. (Membership in the IFMA is a good recommendation.) Some very able speakers represent works that are highly questionable. If you are not sure, investigate. And don't invite the speaker until you are satisfied. (One pastor wrote us asking about a mission after he had completed arrangements for it to hold a conference in his church.) It is easier to keep them out than to explain to the people later.

(2) Mission secretaries, deputation representatives, etc. There are many times when these are to be preferred to the missionary on furlough. In fact, many of them are experienced missionaries who have been kept at home for this special ministry. They are usually effective speakers. These are the speakers to invite if you want a broad picture of the whole work of their mission. The missionary on furlough speaks principally of his own sta-

tion and his personal experiences, but he doesn't always see how they fit into the whole program.

(3) Accepted candidates

Many churches pay scant attention to accepted missionary candidates. They haven't been on the field yet; they only know it at second-hand; so what kind of message can they bring? The answer is simply this: they can bring the inspiration of their example. If they are wise enough to make much of their personal testimony of the Lord's guidance, you will find that they will lead some of the young people to wonder if perhaps they might not be usable on the mission field, too. And they will move older people to deeper devotion by their example of youthful consecration. Even where they are not given a whole church service, you can give them a few minutes very profitably.

b. For what services?

This is largely a matter for the discretion of the pastor or leader. However, to get the greatest profit you will want to have a good missionary speaker at a time when the most people will be able to hear him. Don't use him as bait to increase attendance at an otherwise poorly attended service. He may increase the attendance somewhat, but the blessings of his ministry will be lost to those who didn't get there. And they are often the ones who need it most. And don't overlook the possibility of having him minister in the Sunday school and the Young People's society. But by all means let him know ahead of time if he is to minister there.

c. When to invite

Invite your missionary speaker as much in advance as possible. Even when they live in your city you will sometimes find that their schedules are filled for several months ahead. And if they come from a distance you will want to reduce transportation costs by inviting them when they are planning to be somewhere in your neighborhood. That means your invitation should reach them when they are planning their itinerary. When a missionary responds that he will be able to be with you on a certain date, and that date is acceptable, be sure to confirm it in writing. That way there won't be any slip-up.

d. Financial arrangements

These are sometimes hard to make, because the missionary hesitates to put a certain price on his services as if he were a professional man. These suggestions should help:

(1) Give at least what you would give to a regular pulpit supply, if the missionary takes a church service.

(2) If he comes from a distance, see that his transportation is cared for.

(3) If he has to stay overnight, take care at least of his lodging.

(4) Faith missionaries will not ask for renumeration and may even request that no collection be taken. However, this doesn't prevent your doing what we have mentioned above. Neither does it prevent your putting an offering plate near the door, into which the people may drop an offering if they wish. There should be no outward pressure to give.

(5) In some other cases churches like to take a free-will offering for the missionary in addition to, or in the place of, the regular church offering.

e. Instructions to the speaker

Even the experienced missionary speaker likes to be told precisely what you expect of him.

(1) Be sure to tell him the exact time of the meeting, the length of time for the message, and the type of service it is to be. If your people don't like the service to run overtime, let him know. Some missionaries need this reminder.

(2) Tell him how to reach the church, and if you are arranging accommodations for him, let him know it.

(3) If you want him to use pictures of any sort, find out if he will have his own equipment and let him know what you can provide.

(4) If you don't want a sermon, tell him so. Don't blame the missionary for not giving a missionary talk in a Sunday morning service, if you didn't tell him what you wanted.

f. Conduct of the service

(1) Make sure the missionary's time is not cut short by lengthy announcements and other needless preliminaries. If you want his message give him the full time to deliver it.

(2) Lengthy introductions are unnecessary. Say just enough to tell the people who he is and to whet their appetites to hear him. Then sit down. The longer you talk the less time he has for his message.

(3) If you can't be there, be sure someone capable is in charge. The speaker finds it very awkward to have to direct the service as well as give the message in a strange church.

g. Hospitality

There are two aspects to the problem of providing lodging and board for the missionary speaker. From his point of view it is easier to relax if he is given a room in a hotel and gets his meals at a restaurant. But, aside from the money involved, staying in a

Christian home gives him an opportunity for a unique ministry within the family.

This personal and familiar contact with the missionary is of great benefit to both parties. Many a family has testified of the blessing the missionary has been in the home; while the missionary finds that the family's interest in his work is now on a deeper, more personal basis.

The ideal host takes care of his guest, but in such a way that he doesn't feel burdensome or obligated.

3. Use of audio-visual aids

There was a time when the curios he brought back were the missionary's only visual aids in telling his story. Later he could show photographs, and later still the old black-and-white or hand-colored glass slides. It was left for the present generation to multiply these visual aids and add to them some of the advantages of sound.

It is seldom that a church is prepared to care properly for a missionary museum. Missionaries have found to their sorrow that curios left with the home church tend to disappear, or else they gather dust in some neglected corner. It takes the missionary himself to use them and make them live.

However, there are many newer aids that you can sometimes use, in the absence of the missionary, with real effect. Most important are slides, filmstrips and moving pictures, either with or without sound.

To find out what ones are available and on what conditions, get in touch with the mission board. Sometimes there is a small rental fee, while at others a free-will offering is requested.

Slides and filmstrips sometimes come provided with a lecture that you read as you show the pictures. At other times they have an accompanying record that you can play while you show the pictures. You may have to book moving pictures a good while in advance. They also call for an experienced operator.

These aids do require that the church own or rent equipment if you are going to use them when the missionary is not around. Of course churches are using such equipment more and more commonly in all of their work.

For slides and filmstrips a 300-watt projector is usually strong enough for the average church. A projector that can take both slides and filmstrip is preferred. Automatic slide changers are a great help and do protect the slides but they add to the cost of the machine. The best screen is usually a beaded type, either portable or permanently attached to the ceiling of the room where you show the pictures.

Motion pictures call for more expensive equipment. Of course you can use the same screen, but you need a good 16-millimeter sound projector. If the picture is not a sound picture you can still show it on the sound projector; but you can't show sound film on a silent projector.

A further word about the effective use of these aids. A common mistake in the use of pictures is to expect the pictures to do the whole job alone. It doesn't work. The pictures may be the heart of the program but you need to plan the whole program carefully so that they will have their full effect. Your opening remarks should prepare the way for the pictures and can be as long as you think necessary for that purpose. But your remarks after the pictures should be as brief and to the point as you can make them, perhaps pointing the way to what action should be taken in the light of what you have just seen. *But, no preaching!*

There are several other audio-visual aids that we ought also to mention briefly. You can get flannelgraph stories from the mission fields from several missions, and you can also buy them in Christian bookstores. They are particularly useful for children's meetings. You can also get recordings of missionary stories in Christian bookstores. Then, an increasing number of missionaries are taking tape recorders to the field and are sending home recordings. These are not yet available on a large scale, and the quality is not of the best, but people appreciate them a great deal when they are well acquainted with the missionary.

4. The missionary library
The church that gives serious attention to a church library never has reason to complain of the results. No other investment pays such valuable dividends for so small an amount invested. If it doesn't work out well you will find the cause in one of these three things: either you didn't have a dependable librarian at all times, or your choice of books was poor, or you weren't willing to spend money for new books and to keep the library up. The biggest problem is the librarian, unless the church has a full-time secretary who can handle this matter. It needs someone who is really interested and will be faithful to the task, someone who will keep accurate records and be available at regular times for the borrowing and returning of books.

The biggest mistake in the choice of books is to get those you think the people ought to read rather than those they want to read. You may have to have a certain number of reference works, but most of the books should be of the sort that nearly everybody is interested in reading. When one person likes a book he is sure to recommend it to someone else. But remember that tastes differ.

Of course no library will continue to be used if it doesn't continue to add to its list. Some of these can be gifts from interested friends, which are usually the older books, but you should add new ones constantly, too. To know what books to buy, unless you read them yourself, consult the reviews in some dependable Christian magazine. Publicize these books, too, so that people will want to read them. If you have a bulletin board available, you can put the jacket of the book on the board, together with a review of it.

What *missionary* books should go into the library? If your library is small you will want very few reference works and serious study books. The larger the library, the more of these you may include. A large part of the books will probably be in the nature of missionary stories and biography. Here is an annotated list which we believe will be interesting and useful. It contains books for children as well as for adults.

Children

Aunt Theresa's Missionary Stories (three booklets)
Stories told in popular KYB Club on radio station WMBI.

Forty Missionary Stories, Margaret Eggleston
A popular collection for children.

Jungle Doctor series (nine books), Paul White
Outstanding stories by a medical missionary to Africa.

Year of the Tiger, John Bechtel
Fiction. A touching story of life in China for older children.

Cannibal Country, Charles Ludwig

Big Peanuts, Lucilda Newton
Stories of East Africans by authors who have lived there.

STORIES OF MISSIONARY WORK

Mountains Singing, Sanna Barlow
   Experiences getting missionary recordings of Philippine tribes.

Under a Thatched Roof in a Brazilian Jungle, Rosemary Cunningham
   A missionary family's life in an Amazonian jungle.

Nests Above the Abyss, Isobel Kuhn
   Lisu tribespeople of southwest China receive the Gospel.

Sand and Stars, Ruth Stull
   South American experiences by a popular missionary speaker.

The Blood Hunters and *Gongs in the Night,* Mr. and Mrs. Gordon H. Smith.
   Among the tribespeople of Indo-China.

Cheng's Mother, Irene Forsythe Hanson
   Delightful story of a Chinese Christian by her adopted daughter.

Adventures with God, Jenny de Mayer
   An unusual missionary in little-known lands of the Middle East.

Blossom of the Crag and *Lin of Willow Valley,* Marie Barham
   Well-told tales from China by a missionary of the C.I.M.

BIOGRAPHY

The Moffats, Ethel Daniels Hubbard
   Masterful brief biography of a famous missionary couple.

Hudson Taylor's Spiritual Secret, Dr. and Mrs. F. Howard Taylor
   A blessing for those who haven't time for the two-volume life of Hudson Taylor.

C. T. Studd, Cricketer and Pioneer, Norman P. Grubb
Ever-popular story of an unusual missionary figure.
Rees Howells, Intercessor, Norman P. Grubb
A new biography of a somewhat different sort.
Bible Agent in Spain, Walter McCleary
Condensed account of experiences of George Borrow.
Personal Life of David Livingstone, D. Blaikie
Still considered the best biography of the renowned missionary.
These Sought a Country, K. S. Latourette
Key missionary figures by the foremost historian of missions.
William Carey, F. Deaville Walker
Recently republished account of "the father of modern missions."

Brief biographies by Basil Miller deal with many missionaries.

Missionary Principles and History

The Foreign Missionary, Arthur J. Brown
Still the most interesting and comprehensive book on the subject.
In Training, Rowland Hogben
How to prepare for missionary service.
Ambassadors for Christ, Mildred Cable and Francesca French
What a real missionary should be and do.
The Bible Basis of Missions, Robert H. Glover
Valuable studies by a well-known missionary doctor, teacher and leader.
World Missions, Martha Moennich
General survey based on personal visits.
The Progress of World-Wide Missions, Robert H. Glover
Still a most readable history and survey, though not now up-to-date.

CHAPTER XXIV

A CHURCH MISSIONARY PROGRAM
(*Continued*)

---

5. The missionary conference

One of the most popular means for stirring up missionary interest in a church is the missionary conference. Here in a period of a few days the church centers its whole attention on missions. Such a concentrated effort is usually productive, whether in the raising of the church's missionary budget or in getting young people to volunteer for missionary service. But much of the value of the conference depends on the understanding and care with which you make the plans and on your choice of speakers.

Where only one mission is concerned, as in many of the denominational churches, the church's part in the planning is fairly simple. Since the mission has had experience in such things, after you agree on the date you can allow it to take charge. Of course there will have to be consultation about the details, but the mission will recommend the over-all plan with the selection of speakers. To help carry out the plan is the responsibility of the church.

But where several missions are to be represented, the whole responsibility rests on the church. And it is such conferences that are the most common. They are held even in many denominational churches. We shall give rather extended treatment to this type because its problems will include also the ones you will find in the other.

a. In planning a missionary conference, the first thing is to settle on a time for it. There is no particular time of year that is always better than any other time. Most churches avoid the summer months, but spring, fall and even winter months are commonly used. The Christmas season is avoided, but Easter time is popular. Often the church plans to have the conference near the beginning or end of its fiscal year, with an eye on the budget.

The length of time for the conference is a knotty problem. Local conditions have much to do with it. The choice usually runs from three days to a week. Very few churches find it profitable to run over a week. Sometimes the conference begins with a Sunday and runs through the mid-week prayer meeting. At other times it begins with the mid-week prayer meeting and ends with the Sunday meetings. Another variation has been adopted where it has been difficult to get people out on week nights. A missionary month has been set aside, with missionary speakers at each Sunday and mid-week service during the month. This plan does not have the concentrated impact of the other, but it may reach more people and does sustain the emphasis over a longer period.

b. Local conditions will determine how many and what services you can best use. The plan that works well in one place may not be at all suitable for another. Consider the following:

(1) Most people will attend the regular services. This means that you will have your largest services at

the regular Sunday meeting times, with perhaps the second largest at the mid-week prayer meeting hour. People are used to going to church at these times, and even an exceptionally good speaker may not draw them out at any other time.

(2) The evening services, except on Sunday, will be better attended than afternoon or morning meetings. This doesn't mean that you can't hold profitable daytime meetings in some places. There are people who can and will arrange their work so as to be free to attend such meetings, and of course they are likely to be the ones most deeply interested. But in any case the attendance will be smaller than at night.

(3) Sunday afternoon meetings are often poorly attended in cities, where there are many other attractions. This is something that is very unpredictable. Sometimes Sunday afternoon meetings are very well attended and very profitable.

(4) A word of warning about meetings held at times not in the usual church schedule. Don't make them long! Some people don't mind, but many others do. They won't come out night after night if they think the meetings are too prolonged. Better to have them wish they were longer than feel that they are too long.

(5) Include the Sunday School, Young People's Society, Women's Society and any other church organizations in your plans. The Women's Society may have to move its meeting up a week, but it is usually glad to do so. The Sunday School may want a few words from a missionary in its opening assembly, or to have missionaries speak to the individual classes or groups of classes.

(6) Usable types of meetings

    (a) The Sunday morning service usually follows the regular form, except that a missionary is in the pulpit with a missionary message. The Sunday evening meeting is often varied.

    (b) Where more than one missionary is available for a meeting, you may give one of them part of the time to show pictures, while the other follows with a message. Or vice versa.

    (c) Sometimes it is good to follow a talk with a question period, when the audience is invited to ask the speaker questions. This usually works best in the smaller meetings. Sometimes it is hard to get the people started asking. Let them know ahead of time that there will be such a period, so they can get set for it. And be prepared to get the ball rolling by asking questions yourself.

    (d) Round table or panel discussions are often very valuable if several missionaries are present. It takes a capable and well-informed leader to handle them properly, though.

        In the one, the missionaries discuss one or more problems among themselves, with the audience listening in. The audience, however, may also be allowed to interject questions if it wants to.

        In the other, the questions come from the audience and are referred to one or another of the missionaries on the panel for answer. If the leader or one of the others is not satisfied with an answer, he may give another point of view or add to the answer.

Sometimes leaders "plant" questions in the audience to be asked at the proper time. While this is not always objectionable, there are many who dislike its artificiality. In most cases the "planted" questions are so stereotyped that it is obvious that they didn't originate with the person asking them. With young people keenly interested in missions these discussion periods are very popular.

(e) You ought to plan for special services for the children, and sometimes for the young people. Costumes, curios, stories and songs interest the children. Pictures are good if they are adapted to the children, though this is not usually the case. For the young people you may want to plan the meeting in connection with a picnic or a banquet. Or if there is a Saturday night youth rally, it can be made a missionary rally.

(f) Don't overlook the possibility that one or more of the missionary speakers might be used in the local school or in some civic group. It calls for a speaker with tact and judgment, but in this way you are spreading the blessing beyond your own church. Also, it is good publicity for your meetings.

(7) Exhibits

Leave the planning of exhibits to the missionaries. But notify them well in advance if you want them to provide exhibits. Tell them also how much space they will have, and be sure to have tables available for them.

You will also need tables for displays of literature by the missions represented.

(8) Finances

The same suggestions for contacting speakers apply here as for any other meetings, except that more advance notice may be needed. The financial arrangements, however, may be quite different. They are complicated by the fact that the missionary conference is sometimes used to help raise the annual budget for missions. In such a case it is usually best to plan a stated amount for each speaker, all offerings above that amount going into the church's missionary treasury. However, many churches use another plan. They pay the expenses of the conference from the offering, then divide the remainder proportionately among the missionaries taking part, or their missions.

CHAPTER XXV

A CHURCH MISSIONARY PROGRAM
(*Continued*)

II. Accurate and up-to-date information

Many things we mentioned for stirring up interest serve just as well to keep up that interest. But here we want to add several items more.

1. Bulletin board

In many active missionary churches you will find a special missionary bulletin board. It has a variety of uses. Pictures and letters from the fields sometimes appear on it. Sometimes it carries special announcements of missionary meetings or a copy of the church missionary budget. It is a good place to advertise a new missionary book. It all depends on the alertness of the one in charge. Perhaps we don't need to add that it loses its value if you don't keep it up.

If the church has missionaries of its own, it needs to keep them before the people. "Out of sight, out of mind" applies here. The missionary is gone for three to seven years at a stretch. Meantime the church membership is changing. Perhaps a new pastor comes. And even those who do remember the missionary find their recollections somewhat vague. Whether on the bulletin board or in some other prominent spot, each missionary's picture should find a permanent place. With it should be his name and postal address.

2. Map

Some people find maps very dull. But that is either because they haven't learned to read them or because they haven't much interest in what the map shows. Maps are like pictures. They try to help us visualize what an area looks like if we could see it all at once. Primitive people often have trouble trying to "see" a picture. Just so, those who are not used to maps have to learn to read them and "see" what they picture.

But most Americans can read a map that is not too detailed. In fact, if they are at all interested in a place they like to get a general idea of where it is. That's why newspapers so often print small outline maps with news items from abroad. It helps to locate them.

Just so, the church should help its people to locate their missionaries or mission fields. It doesn't take a detailed map. The simpler the better for most people. But a general map on which you can make the place you are interested in stand out is a real help. Put it where they can see it.

3. Missionary letters

The most up-to-date news from the mission fields comes through missionary letters. Of course such news comes in small bits. And it isn't always important. Most missionaries write about their own station and work and don't give the broad view. They leave that to others. But it's from these bits of news that you can put the whole picture together.

If the church is helping support a missionary on the field, it will usually hear from him with fair regularity. He usually acknowledges its gifts. Here is where churches often make a mistake. The letter sometimes gets no farther than the pastor or the treasurer to whom it is addressed. No one else sees it, unless it be the Women's Missionary Society. No one thinks of answering it. Money was sent; a letter comes in acknowledgment; and that's that.

But that shouldn't be all. The money was from the church, so the church should see the letter—at least those parts which interest it. Here's where the missionary bulletin board comes in handy. Post the letters there where anyone who wants may read them.

And go a step farther. Answer the letters. There are pastors at home who have never taken the time to write a letter to their missionary. They hear from him. In fact they would think him very remiss if he didn't write. But they are "just too busy" to answer. We're not going to scold the pastor. He probably *is* busy. (So is the missionary.) But he is missing an opportunity to minister, just as if he skipped making a needed pastoral call on one of his members. And he's making it harder for the missionary to write as freely as he would like.

The pastor isn't the only one concerned. Letters come to the treasurer and others which are never answered. Let someone be responsible for answering them. It doesn't have to be the same one every time, but it should be a clear-cut responsibility. A general request in the church bulletin for the members to write to their missionary is too vague. Hardly anyone will write. Put the duty on a specific person. He is more likely to do it, and he will get a blessing from it.

Speaking of the church bulletin, if you have one, here is a good place to publish occasional extracts from missionary letters. Most church bulletins are too monotonous, anyway. Here's a way to add variety and interest. And the people will read them. They'll read them much more than they would if they saw them tacked on the bulletin board.

So far we have talked only about the personal letters the missionary writes. We haven't mentioned form letters. Whether you think the missionaries are overdoing this form-letter business or not, it is a fixed part of modern missions. The missionary would like to write to so many people, and there are so many people who want to hear from him, that a form letter seems to be the only answer. Usually they are mimeographed.

Every pastor is likely to receive a number of these form letters from different missionaries. You don't have to answer them unless you want to. But they do give news that you may be able to use. In fact, some denominational missions do the mimeographing for their missionaries. Then they can run off extra copies and send packets of them to churches that are interested. They are much more informal than magazine articles.

These form letters are usually sent to all who ask for them, or to anyone who has shown a real interest in the missionary and his work. But in his home church he faces a problem. Should he try to send a letter to every member? It's a lot of work and expense for the already overburdened worker. Here the church itself steps in. It says to the missionary, "Send us your letter, and we'll see that every one of our members gets a copy." This is not only a help to the missionary, it ties him in more closely with the church in the minds of the people. And this is as it should be. Besides, it keeps the members informed.

4. Magazines

For a greater amount of news in a smaller space we need the missionary magazine. Each mission has its own magazine. Some are monthly, some bi-monthly, some quarterly. Some are well edited; others are merely collections of missionary letters. Some have a stated subscription price; others are sent out free of charge. But all deal almost entirely with the work of the mission which publishes them.

We are sorry to say that since 1939, when the *Missionary Review of the World* stopped publication, no general missionary magazine has been published in the United States. The reason is financial—too few subscribers and no subsidies. Most people are concerned with their own group, and in most cases their gifts help cover the costs of its magazine. There are, however, some Christian magazines like *Moody Monthly* which give a certain amount of space each month to general missionary news and interests.

Two British publications deserve mention. The *International Review of Missions* is a quarterly sponsored by the International Missionary Council. It has its values but is too technical for the average Christian reader. *World Dominion,* a bi-monthly published by World Dominion Press, is more readable and varied. But its circulation in this country has not been large.

What should the church do about missionary magazines? We recommend three things. First, the library. The church library should be receiving the regular denominational papers. It should also have at least one Christian magazine of a more general nature in which there will be some coverage of missions. It should receive regularly the mission magazine of each mission in which the church has an interest.

Second, promote circulation. The church itself profits when it urges its members to get one or more of these magazines for themselves. An informed church is an active church. The two go together. In some cases a special price is offered if a number of copies are sent to one address. Of course, if there is no subscription price the problem is just distributing the papers. The most economical way is just to announce that they will be available at the door as the congregation leaves a Sunday service. But the economical way is not always the best.

Third, encourage reading. Circulation is not enough if the people don't read what they get. And in these days of much printing we skip a great deal in our reading. Yet much of what we skip we might read if some friend were to recommend it or stir up our interest in it. So those who lead in the church's missionary program will do well to recommend articles of special interest. But don't just say they are interesting. Tell why they are important to read. Better still, give just a taste so that people will want to know more.

III. Prayer support

It scarcely seems necessary to say more about the missionary's need for our prayers. We know he needs prayer and counts on it. Yet we don't take many practical measures to provide it. That is, as a church we don't.

Many are familiar with the story of the missionary who had to leave his field unexpectedly. Reaching his home town on a Wednesday evening, he decided to drop in on the church prayer meeting. Quietly he took a seat in the rear and listened. During the whole service not a word about missions—not a prayer for the missionaries! He knew then why the going had been so hard.

This little story highlights the need to pray for missionaries in the prayer meeting. But the need is broader than that. It is a need for the prayers of the whole church—of all the members who know how to pray. It is part of the church's ministry, and a part in which every member can take a part.

How to get such prayers? It takes deliberate planning. You can't do it by simply urging everyone to pray, "Lord, bless the missionaries." We pray for people when we know they have a real need. The greater the need, the more likely we are to pray. The problem then is to get the people to see the need.

The missionaries themselves are sometimes at fault here. They hesitate to make their needs known. Or sometimes they state them in such general terms you don't know just exactly what they do need and why. I don't mean physical needs; those are usually pretty clear. But we are all rather shy about revealing our spiritual needs. Yet they may be just as great. We are often afraid that they may show up our weakness, or the weakness of our work.

Of course there are many needs that are not purely personal and don't affect just the work of the one missionary. The religious persecution of believers, natural calamities such as floods, or the inroads of false cults, all call for prayer. And the missionary is usually not hesitant in asking prayer for different members of his flock.

The problem is to present the known needs in such a way that people will pray at home as well as in church. The prayer meeting is the natural place, but it reaches only a small part of the people. A pastoral announcement and prayer on Sunday morning will alert many more. Of course the missionary society should be interested. But why not the Sunday School, too? And you can often get more sincere, unselfish praying in a young people's society than anywhere else.

Sometimes the church will issue a missionary prayer list. If it does so the requests should be clear cut and definite. Give enough information so people will know why they are asked to pray. And when answers come, report them. There don't need to be many requests. It is better to concentrate on a very few important ones. You will get more co-operation.

CHAPTER XXVI

A CHURCH MISSIONARY PROGRAM
(*Continued*)

IV. Material support

We have said that the church should give material support in as large a measure as possible. Don't ask how large a measure that is. I don't know. All I can say is that I never knew a church that was doing all it could. Yet I have known some very generous ones. The experience of those churches that have increased their giving year by year shows that there is always room for improvement.

The measure of a church's giving is not the number of its members. Some of the largest churches are the poorest givers. And we may add that some of the wealthiest churches are put to shame in their giving by some of the poorest. The thing is not to measure ourselves by what others are doing but to ever improve our own position.

For this reason we always do well to set an objective. Make it high enough so that it will not be easy to reach—it ought to be a challenge. But don't make it so high that reaching it is out of the question and the people will get discouraged. People are stirred to greater efforts when they have a definite, reachable goal.

And let the people know just what they are giving for. If there is any item on your missionary budget that you don't want the members to see, it shouldn't be there! There is no surer way to discourage giving than to keep the budget secret.

Sometimes churches are puzzled to know whether they should support only missionaries who are their own members. The answer is not as hard as some make it seem. Of course you should support your own members first of all. That is, if they are not out of fellowship with the church. They are your representatives on the mission field in a way in which others could not be. They are a part of you. They are your responsibility.

Then, if you are able to give more, or if you have no one from your church on the mission field, give to others. The only question here is whether it is better to give full support to one or part support to several. There are advantages both ways. Let the church decide.

But if the members of the church who go out as missionaries are more than the church can support, the problem is more serious. Even one missionary is more than some churches can support. What then? The only possible answer is this. Keep up your support of those already on your list. Take on the support of the newer ones as fast as you are able. Don't drop the ones nor neglect the others. Let the new missionaries needing support be a challenge to greater efforts in giving. But under no conditions drop the older missionaries so as to support the new ones.

There is a practice that sometimes afflicts our independent churches. I saw it first in the experience of one missionary couple about twenty years ago. In the middle of their second term of service, their two supporting churches, in different parts of the country, both announced that they were dropping their support. They had other interests. There was nothing the missionaries could do.

Such a thing usually happens when there is a change of pastor. The new pastor is not acquainted with the church's missionaries. He may have some favorite missionary projects of his own. So he begins to push his own program and gets the church to drop the old one. Not long ago a new pastor was called to a large independent church. One of the missionaries supported by the church was a young woman who had grown up in it. For years the church had been an active supporter of the mission with which she worked. But now things changed. After a time the young woman got notice that the church was reducing the amount of her support. Its gifts for missions had not decreased; in fact they were increasing. But the church had some other plans . . .

This fault is not the only one the church needs to guard against. Another is the temptation to seek bargains in missions. Recently a young candidate told me his home church might not be willing to support him on the field. "They told me," he said, "that if I would go to another field it wouldn't cost so much."

Maybe not. Maybe we ought to use "good business sense" and spend all our missionary money where we can "get the most for it." Maybe we ought to withdraw our missionaries from the barren Mohammedan fields and send them where results are easier to get. Maybe—but if we do we are turning our backs on the greatest of all missionaries, Jesus Christ. Look at what His mission cost Him! We are commercializing the consecration of our young people. They are spending their lives. We are trying to count the value of human souls in dollars and cents.

There are no bargains in missions. You get no more than what you pay for by sacrificial effort. "He that soweth sparingly shall reap also sparingly."

What does it cost to support a missionary? It depends. Better ask the mission. But this I can say, many missionary men are receiving less than a street car conductor, and many women are paid less than a stenographer fresh out of high school. Why? Because the church doesn't give more.

"But it doesn't cost so much to live in other countries," some will object.

You're wrong. In many places it costs more, *if you try to*

keep up the same standard of living. What happens is that the missionary learns to do without many of the things we enjoy at home. It just makes it easier that the people around him don't have them either.

The temptation to find bargains in missions makes some take up the idea of supporting native workers. The native can evangelize his own people better than the missionary. The missionary himself admits it. And in some cases he can be supported for a fraction of the cost of a missionary. So why not spend our money supporting native workers?

The missionaries themselves started this idea. Now they have to face it. Some are still spreading it, but more and more they are turning away from it. Over and over they have found that it doesn't work out in practice.

The first part of the argument is sound. The native *can* evangelize his own people better than the missionary in many cases. Often he *can* be supported for less than the cost of a missionary. But the conclusion doesn't follow. We still *have to* have the missionaries.

Let's put it this way. A certain factory hires 200 workmen to manufacture its product. Besides these 200 there are a number of supervisors, a large office force and several top officials. One day an agitator gets hold of some of the workmen. "Why should those officials get so much more money than you do?" he says. "You're the ones who do the work! What's the use of all those white-collar workers? It's you workmen who produce!"

It sounds right to the workers. But get rid of those others and what do you have? Only one word can describe it—chaos. Supplies dwindle; finished products pile up in the warehouse with no one to buy them; faulty pieces reach the consumer and break down in use; bills pile up; credit is gone; the factory has to close its doors.

The missionaries will be needed until they have nationals trained to take over the whole of the work, not just the preaching. We have said that native workers can evangelize their own people better than missionaries. This is not because they are better workers. It is largely because a foreigner always works under a handicap. People always listen more readily to one of themselves, one whose previous life they may have known and whose way of speaking has a familiar sound.

But native workers have to be converted first. Then they have to develop in Christian experience. And if they are to give full time to Christian work they must be trained. All of this means work for the missionary. But it isn't the end. The workers must be directed and supervised in their work. They must be counseled, occasionally rebuked, and sometimes discharged. Or would you be willing to hire a worker, sight unseen, and support him regularly in the vague hope that he will do good work without supervision? Some churches are actually doing it! And they have come to regret it.

Still, this is not what is turning the missionaries away from the hiring of native workers. It is something even more fundamental. While native workers can do a good job of evangelism, this doesn't mean native workers *hired with foreign funds*. Especially not today. We Americans are constantly being accused of trying to buy people with our money. So the native worker we hire is at once under suspicion. He is the American's hired man.

But let's go a little deeper. The hiring of native workers with American funds has seemed a good way of multiplying our ministry. We have usually thought of it as temporary. Through these workers a church would soon be built up, and then the mission could withdraw its support and the church would take over. It was all very logical. But it didn't work. Two or three generations later we would still find the workers supported by American funds. And not too many workers at that. The church also seemed very weak.

Missionaries have been learning that the so-called indigenous principles are the only sound principles on which to build a lasting work. The word indigenous simply means native. In its simplest form it means that the church is to be native from the beginning. The natives are expected to spread the Gospel and win members for the church; they are to pay all the expenses of the church; and they are to run the church. The terms most often used are: self-propagation, self-support, and self-government.

We'll not go into the details of these principles. But we want to call attention to the fact that the natives are to win their fellows, which we said is good. But they are also to pay the expenses. That means no money from American churches for their support.

There is only one reason why the missionaries have opposed using American money to pay native workers. In the long run it hinders the church. There is no question about it. It has been proved over and over. One large mission adopted the policy some years ago of refusing to accept gifts for designated native workers. They would accept undesignated gifts to be used only at the mission's discretion. They were trying to shift the responsibility to the church itself.

After a few years the mission was able to report that the church was growing faster than ever before in the mission's history. Besides—and this seemed to surprise them—*the number of natives engaged in the work was many times what it was before*. In other words, they got more workers when they stopped putting them on the American payroll. It didn't happen immediately. It took time. But the end result was excellent.

What place does the missionary have in such a program? Just the place that Paul had in New Testament days. He introduces the Gospel and welcomes the first converts; he helps the church get started and begins their instruction in the Word; he counsels and admonishes them and is constant in prayer for them; he shows them how, but theirs is the responsibility for carrying on the work of the church. And he trusts there will come a day when he, like Paul, can say, "I have no more room in these parts" (see Rom. 15:23). As some have said, "The missionary's job is to work himself out of a job."

When we said the church's objective is "to provide material support" for missions, we didn't mean just money. Money is the most widely useful. But sometimes you can do a great deal in other ways.

Of course some will think immediately of the "missionary barrel." The barrel isn't used as much as it used to be. In other days churches gathered all sorts of items, useful and otherwise, and sent them off to missionaries in faraway places. Some things were for the missionary and his family, others to be distributed among the people. The arrival of the barrel was always an exciting event. No one could ever foretell what might be in it. But in most fields such shipments are no longer welcomed. High tariff barriers have been raised by so many countries that the missionary may have to pay in duty several times what the shipment is worth.

So if you are thinking of sending your missionary a package —big or little—think again. Don't send it until you have checked with him. Then follow his instructions. You can't send him a surprise package this way, but better no surprise than a tariff that will cost him dearly. There is no way of pre-paying duty charges.

But when the missionary is at home you can readily give him things that will be useful on the field. He will be glad to tell you what he can use. Only remember this, if you are buying new items at retail, you might do better to give the missionary the money and let him buy them. You see, he often is in touch with Christian dealers who will supply the goods at wholesale. Of course you will not give him used articles unless they are in tip-top condition.

The same thing applies to new missionaries whom you are helping with their outfit. The one difference is that the new missionary doesn't know exactly what he will need. He has to depend on an outfit list supplied by the mission.

Whether giving money or goods, there is one error to avoid. Don't give as if dispensing charity. And make sure that the congregation does not get that impression. Give as to a faithful worker who is worthy of his hire. He is the Lord's servant; give as to the Lord himself.

CHAPTER XXVII

A CHURCH MISSIONARY PROGRAM
(*Continued*)

V. Personnel

Most churches are inclined to think of the missionary enterprise as something apart from themselves. This is especially true when we talk about getting missionary candidates. Missionaries have to come from somewhere. They know that. But it hasn't occurred to them that some of their own young people might be missionary material. It hasn't occurred to them because nobody has suggested it. No one has challenged their young people with the need for just what they have to offer— the unselfish devotion and service of their lives.

The church is really the natural recruiting ground for missions. It is the one place where you will find nearly all of the young people who are interested in Christianity. Some of them have been reared in the church, some were converted there, but practically all come to the church for Christian worship and fellowship. They may not all be truly Christian. They may be there just because it is the proper thing to do. But at least they are susceptible to Christian teaching and they are in the place where they would naturally expect it to be given.

What are you doing with the young people in your church? Do you have any definite aims and program for them? Not just for missions. That will come if your spiritual program is a vital one. But are you paying serious attention to your young people? Do you have some goals that you are earnestly trying to help them reach?

For we can't have missionaries until we have consecrated young Christians. Yes, and instructed Christians, too. The entertainment of our young people is not the church's major task, though some act as if they thought so. Merely to keep them in some sort of association with the church is not enough. A vital program means spiritual guidance. It means bringing them into a living relationship with the Lord and with His Word. It means trying to get them to accept His Lordship in deciding the course of their lives, whatever their line of work. And that is not easy. Neither are all ministers willing or capable of doing it.

What can the churches do about providing personnel for missions? For one thing, they can repeatedly challenge young Christians to such a service for their Lord. But before that step can mean much, they must lay a foundation.

Young people should be finding their Saviour in the church. Then, step by step, they should be going on into a deeper knowledge and experience of Him. And periodically they should be faced there with the need to dedicate their lives to Him. The regularly recurring "consecration meeting" of the Christian Endeavor movement had a sound idea behind it. Then challenge them to offer their lives for service abroad.

Of course confronting young people with such a challenge is also a part of our first objective, that of stimulating missionary interest in the church. But here you have a special group in mind. When you issue the challenge for missions, you are aiming at the young people. Few older ones could go. And you will often find the young people more responsive than you think. Young people are idealists. This in spite of the carping criticism of "the younger generation" by disillusioned middle-agers. They are more ready to give their lives for an ideal than are their elders.

Challenge them first of all to a full dedication to Christ. They are Christians. Remind them that they are the ones whom "he hath purchased with his own blood." Tell them that "he died for all, that they which live should not henceforth live unto themselves, but unto him which died for them, and rose again."

Such full dedication doesn't necessarily mean "full-time Christian service." But it may. It may even mean foreign missionary service. But we don't stress it for that reason. We stress it because no Christian can be fully effective without it. We stress it because we don't want missionary candidates who are not first of all dedicated whole-heartedly to Christ. They must be first dedicated to Christ and then to missions, not the other way around.

Then challenge them to look on the world's need and on their own possibilities. The two go together. To know of a need that you can't help to meet is frustrating. To have a gift, an ability or training for which there is no need is just as frustrating. They won't analyze the world's need perfectly. Who can? And they may put too high or too low a value on their own ability to fill the need. But even such a dim vision will give to life the purpose that it needs. We all need to be persuaded that what we are doing really matters.

And finally, challenge them to offer their lives for the Lord to use and to get prepared for whatever He has for them. Note that we don't say "to offer their lives for foreign missions." There is a reason. We do want some of them for foreign missions. But it is much more important that they be ready for anything the Lord has for them. Some people are willing to volunteer if they can choose the type and place of service. But what the Lord wants are those who will put themselves in His hands and say, "Use me where You need me most." It may be in foreign missions. But don't be surprised if it is in a line you never thought of. There is no reason why a Christian businessman should not be as sincerely dedicated to the Lord as any minister or missionary.

And note that we say to challenge them to get prepared. This is often a weak spot. We challenge young people to dedicate their lives to missionary service; but we don't tell them at the same time that it takes dedication to get thoroughly prepared for the job. As a result they are so impatient to "get going" that they slight their preparation or look for short-cuts. Why don't we tell them that they will have to spend time and work getting ready for this great ministry? Are we afraid they will get discouraged? They won't if they are the right kind. Instead, it is likely to increase their respect for the work.

But in your recruiting for missionary service do avoid some of the serious mistakes that are so common today. Let me list five of them.

First is a superficial emotionalism that quickly fades away. We are not discounting emotion. The emotions must be touched. We wouldn't give much for a missionary candidate who didn't feel keenly his call to witness for Christ. Again we say, we would like to have those who feel intensely, as Paul did, "Woe is me if I preach not the gospel!" But the appeal that reaches the heart springs and has an enduring effect is not the same as the one that merely stirs up our feelings for the night. Decisions made in the warm glow of an exciting meeting are often regretted in the gray dawn of reality. So don't whip up an artificial enthusiasm but try to touch the depths of the soul.

Second, avoid the glamorizing of missionary life and work. Any missionary can tell you how quickly the glamour vanishes when you reach the field. To some it comes as a rude shock, for they weren't prepared for the stark reality. Of course you can't help it that so many think all strange lands and people are glamorous. Their very distance from us makes them look romantic. But you can avoid heightening that impression. Put the emphasis where it belongs, on the great motives and purpose of missions, not on the bizarre, the strange and unusual features of missionary life. Remember that even horror can have a romantic attraction. When you tell a missionary story, be careful not to overcolor it.

A third mistake is that of appealing to a sense of pity for the people because of their great physical needs. Such an appeal does have a place. But its place is not that of recruiting young people for the spiritual ministry of missions. Even the nationals of other countries have often protested against this sort of appeal. They remind us that we have paupers and slums in our own country, as well as depraved criminals. They resent an attitude of condescending pity. We don't want our missionaries to go to the field with such an attitude as their main motive.

In the fourth place, there is an unwise tendency to present foreign missionary work as the highest form of heroic consecration. Really it isn't. Many a missionary will assure you that it isn't. Missionaries are often embarrassed by the sort of hero-worship that is heaped upon them unsought and undesired. Not that there isn't a great deal of heroism exhibited in many mission fields. And for some young people it takes a heroic decision to get them out. But for many the decision to tackle an unromantic job at home is even harder. In fact, for some the foreign field looks like a way to escape frustration at home. The highest form of consecration is to deny onself and to take up one's cross and follow Christ—regardless of where He may lead.

A final mistake in recruiting is one that is hardly worthy to be mentioned and yet is quite commonly made. It is the appeal to young people to help enlarge the ministry of their own church, their own denomination, their own mission. This is nothing but selfishness masquerading as Christian missions. We are not of those who oppose denominations. As long as Christianity is a really vital force it is likely to break out in new ways at any time. Regimentation means stagnation. But when any Christian group thinks chiefly of its own perpetuation or enlargement it is getting away from its Christian basis. The shameful competition and overlapping of work in some mission fields is not caused primarily by the fact that we have various denominations. It is caused rather by those who confuse the glory of Christ with the glorification of their own organization. Don't be guilty of inspiring young people to go out with such a vainglorious attitude. Challenge them to preach not themselves but Christ. Try to see that their chief concern is for the honor of Christ and that the world may experience the life of Christ.

But a further word. Don't just challenge. Tell what kinds of missionaries we need. Of course that means that you will need to know, yourself. It means you will have to be interested enough to keep in touch with the mission. Or at times you may prefer to have a missionary or a mission secretary deal with the matter. But do make it definite. Don't encourage those who are clearly inferior. Don't say, "You can probably be used somewhere." Could you use them at home? Don't encourage divorced persons, or those who are overage or "queer," or those who are not willing to work hard to prepare. Don't make candidate secretaries do all the weeding out. You know your young people better than they do. And don't hesitate to encourage some of them individually. They may need just a little encouragement. But don't push. Let the Lord do the calling.

Provide opportunities for your young people to meet missionaries and missionary candidates personally. Just an invitation to speak to the missionary after the service is not enough. Only a few of the more venturesome will do it. Arrange for a discussion group or something similar. Or maybe a small gathering in a home. These personal contacts are valuable. They bring home to your young people, as nothing else could, that missionaries are just ordinary people with an extraordinary devotion to their Saviour.

Again we say, the local church is the natural recruiting ground for missions. Does your church have the vision? Is it meeting the need?

CHAPTER XXVIII

A CHURCH MISSIONARY PROGRAM
(*Concluded*)

VI. Training

Not all the training of missionary candidates is carried on by Bible institutes, seminaries, and other missionary training schools. The local church does its part. And it is not an insignificant part. As we have mentioned before, the most important part of the preparation of missionaries is done outside of the classroom. In fact, all four of the indispensables of missionary preparation can in some measure be provided in the church.

But the church doesn't need to carry on a missionary training program separate from the rest of its program of training young people. It should be just a part of that same program. The church can't give the specialized instruction needed for foreign service. What it can and should do is train its young people to be good witnesses for Christ wherever they are. This is foundational. The special training they need to serve in other lands can be added elsewhere.

Let us take it for granted that the church is sincerely and seriously interested in the development of its young people. It not only wants to see them continue faithful to the church; it desires to help them grow in spirituality and leadership. It hopes to see them make some useful contribution to the work of the church and to the whole cause of Christ. So it is willing to give special attention to the training of its youth. What then, can it do that will be important in missionary training?

Let me mention five things.

First comes the matter of personal consecration and the spiritual life. Every pastor recognizes that this is part of his usual responsibility. Among his Christian young people are some who were reared in the church. Others have come into it out of non-Christian surroundings through conversion. It makes little difference. In every case they need to be brought to the place of personal dedication. Sometimes those who were brought up in Christian surroundings are the hardest to get to see their need of such dedication. But they cannot know the fullness of the Christian life until they make it.

A single act of dedication is not enough. No more so than the single act of joining the church. It should set the course for our life; but, oh, how often we veer away to one side or the other and end up completely off course! We need training in the spiritual life. That is, we not only need to know the principles, but we need to have instruction in applying them to daily living, we need to have practice in doing it. We need to learn how to put first in our lives "the kingdom of God and his righteousness."

Second is the matter of systematic Bible study. This, too, should be a part of the church's usual ministry. Sometimes it is well done. Sometimes any young person who wants to can get in his home church a good broad foundation in the teachings of Scripture. But often this is not so. Especially when most of the Bible teaching is left to the Sunday school and its often haphazard teaching under inexperienced teachers.

This is one of the great values of expository preaching. It is Bible teaching from the pulpit. And since so many never attend any but the preaching services of the church, it is the kind of teaching that helps to raise the whole level of Bible instruction in the church. That is, if it is well done.

But when listening to expository sermons, or even to Bible lectures given at the church's mid-week service, the young people are passive. They listen and drink in—if they want to. But there is no chance for them to clarify their understanding by asking questions. There is no chance for them to express what they are learning, so as to fix it more firmly in their minds.

It is this purpose that the young people's society should fill. It gives the youth of the church a chance to express what they are learning. And there is no surer way for them to fix a teaching in their own minds than to try to teach it to others. It encourages them to search the Scriptures for themselves and discuss its teachings among those of similar age and experience. With good counsel the young people's society can be an invaluable training school. Without such counsel it may become just an insipid social club. Or it may turn into another preaching service where young people are expected just to sit and listen.

But besides these things there is still a need for more systematic and consecutive study of the Bible. The Bible class is needed. It may be a part of the Sunday school. It may be held on some weekday evening. Whatever the arrangement, it is a serious and purposeful attempt to get the fullness of Scripture teaching instead of snatches here and there. Often such a class will make use of a correspondence course such as those that are offered by Moody Bible Institute. Sometimes examinations are given; sometimes not. Only a minority of the church attend, but it is from this interested minority that the missionary candidates as well as church leaders will probably come. And when they get to the training schools, the value of this Bible teaching in the home church is soon apparent.

Personal witnessing is a third field in which the local church can provide training. Perhaps it is more a matter of inspiration and encouragement than it is of instruction. Classes in personal evangelism have their place, but they are not much good without practice. Nothing can take the place of actually talking with men and women about the faith we have in Christ. Many do it spontaneously in the enthusiasm of their new-found faith. But today, when the great majority of our church members have been reared in the faith, this is not the rule. Most young people need to be encouraged to do it and they need to be shown how.

The subject of personal evangelism is too big for us to deal with it here. But we can make one or two suggestions. Young people will usually do better at first if at least two work together. Even if one tends to take the lead and do most of the talking, the other is still learning from their joint experience. Also, to keep up interest in this personal witnessing, there ought to be a chance to tell others about it—to share experiences. Testimony meetings are unheard of in most churches today, and the churches have lost more than they realize by dropping them. The pleasure we take in any experience is greatly increased by telling someone else about it. And if this is true in our personal religious experience, it is doubly so in the matter of witnessing to others.

In the fourth place there are opportunities for leadership and service that the local church can provide. This is extremely important in missionary preparation. It is amazing to see how many young people enter missionary training schools without any previous experience in Christian work. In the case of recent converts to Christianity this is of course understandable. There hasn't been time for them to get such experience. Perhaps we can excuse it, too, on the part of those whose Christianity was largely formal and superficial until shortly before they entered. But there are many others who might have been willing to work but they needed opportunities and guidance—especially guidance.

It is true that a missionary has to learn to take the initiative in such things. Young people who always have to be told what to do don't make good missionaries. But on the other hand, the church leaders don't always welcome initiative on the part of the young people. And they don't always see the leadership possibilities in many of them. As we have said before, leadership is not merely a matter of natural talent. And even where that talent exists, it needs encouragement and guidance.

The wise church deliberately gives responsibility to its young people. And it is not just the responsibility for running their own young people's society. Every bit of Christian service is a part of training—especially where they have to lead others. And in every church there are many services in which the young people could have a part. Of course they often teach Sunday school classes—though they usually need more instruction and counsel for the job than they get. High school boys can develop into very acceptable ushers. Games at the Sunday school picnic, and even other parts of the program, can often be turned over to the young people. Older young people can sponsor younger groups, sometimes with better understanding and greater success than adults would have. Some churches have found it worth while to turn over an occasional evening service to the young people, letting them plan and direct it all except the sermon. Others have encouraged the forming of "Gospel teams" and other such groups who carry their witness to neglected places, to jails, missions and even other churches. And we could extend the list indefinitely. The important thing is that, while the church benefits from their services, these young people are getting invaluable training for missionary service.

One last suggestion has to do with schools. When a young volunteer offers his life for missionary service, he usually knows that he will need to get some special training. But being young and enthusiastic, he doesn't want to spend any longer getting that training than he has to.

It is at this point that his pastor can render a real missionary service. If the pastor has the young person's confidence he can direct him to those schools and courses of training that will best meet his need. He can see to it that he doesn't try to short-cut his preparation. He can tell him where to get the special advice that the pastor himself may not be able to give. He can encourage him to go ahead in spite of difficulties.

One major difficulty that faces many candidates is the financing of their training. Even in schools where no tuition is charged, the student still has many other expenses. Should the church help him? Especially since he is going to be a missionary?

Some do. Some churches include in their budget a certain amount to be used in helping their young people get training for Christian service. They believe it is a sound investment of the Lord's money. And that can be very true.

But there are problems. There are always some who begin their training and never complete it. There are others who finish their training but never enter the service they intended. How is the church going to feel about these young people? Will it condemn them for accepting its help and then not carrying through? Will it make them feel like debtors?

Again, there are some whose choice of a mission board is not what the home church would prefer. But because the church has given them some financial help in their training, they feel obligated to accept the choice of the church or pastor. Or if they don't, they are afraid they will offend the folks back home. Should young people be tied down with financial strings to the choices others make for them?

Such problems can be solved. But we need to face them in order to solve them. Let's face them frankly. Let's urge our young people to follow the Lord's guidance. And then let's show our confidence in Him and them by offering our help with no strings attached. Let them be responsible to Him, not to us, even as we also are responsible to Him. Let His Gospel and the glory of His name be our chief concern, and not our own interests. Only so can we fulfill our missionary obligation.

INDEX